D1104676

Teens and Sex

Other Books of Related Interest:

Opposing Viewpoints Series

AIDS

Sexual Violence

Current Controversies

Health Care

Sex Offenders and Public Policy

At Issue Series

Sexually Transmitted Diseases

CONTEMPORARY
ISSUES
COMPANION

Teens and Sex

David Erik Nelson, Book Editor

GREENHAVEN PRESS
A part of Gale, Cengage Learning

GALE
CENGAGE Learning™

Detroit • New York • San Francisco • New Haven, Conn • Waterville, Maine • London

YA 306.7 T 8|09

GALE
CENGAGE Learning

Christine Nasso, *Publisher*
Elizabeth Des Chenes, *Managing Editor*

ISBN-13: 978-0-7377-3269-6 (hardcover)
ISBN-13: 978-0-7377-3270-2 (pbk.)

Library of Congress Control Number: 2008924777

Printed in the United States of America
2 3 4 5 6 7 12 11 10 09 08

Contents

Foreword

In the news, on the streets, and in neighborhoods, individuals are confronted with a variety of social problems. Such problems may affect people directly: A young woman may struggle with depression, suspect a friend of having bulimia, or watch a loved one battle cancer. And even the issues that do not directly affect her private life—such as religious cults, domestic violence, or legalized gambling—still impact the larger society in which she lives. Discovering and analyzing the complexities of issues that encompass communal and societal realms as well as the world of personal experience is a valuable educational goal in the modern world.

Effectively addressing social problems requires familiarity with a constantly changing stream of data. Becoming well informed about today's controversies is an intricate process that often involves reading myriad primary and secondary sources, analyzing political debates, weighing various experts' opinions—even listening to firsthand accounts of those directly affected by the issue. For students and general observers, this can be a daunting task because of the sheer volume of information available in books, periodicals, on the evening news, and on the Internet. Researching the consequences of legalized gambling, for example, might entail sifting through congressional testimony on gambling's societal effects, examining private studies on Indian gaming, perusing numerous web sites devoted to Internet betting, and reading essays written by lottery winners as well as interviews with recovering compulsive gamblers. Obtaining valuable information can be time-consuming—since it often requires researchers to pore over numerous documents and commentaries before discovering a source relevant to their particular investigation.

Greenhaven's Contemporary Issues Companion series seeks to assist this process of research by providing readers with useful and pertinent information about today's complex issues. Each volume in this anthology series focuses on a topic of current interest, presenting informative and thought-provoking selections written from a wide variety of viewpoints. The readings selected by the editors include such diverse sources as personal accounts and case studies, pertinent factual and statistical articles, and relevant commentaries and over–views. This diversity of sources and views, found in every Contemporary Issues Companion, offers readers a broad perspective in one convenient volume.

In addition, each title in the Contemporary Issues Companion series is designed especially for young adults. The selections included in every volume are chosen for their accessibility and are expertly edited in consideration of both the reading and comprehension levels of the audience. The structure of the anthologies also enhances accessibility. An introductory essay places each issue in context and provides helpful facts such as historical background or current statistics and legislation that pertain to the topic. The chapters that follow organize the material and focus on specific aspects of the book's topic. Every essay is introduced by a brief summary of its main points and biographical information about the author. These summaries aid in comprehension and can also serve to direct readers to material of immediate interest and need. Finally, a comprehensive index allows readers to efficiently scan and locate content.

The Contemporary Issues Companion series is an ideal launching point for research on a particular topic. Each anthology in the series is composed of readings taken from an extensive gamut of resources, including periodicals, newspapers, books, government documents, the publications of private and public organizations, and Internet web sites. In these volumes, readers will find factual support suitable for use in reports, debates, speeches, and research papers. The anthologies also facilitate further research, featuring a book and periodical bibliography and a list of organizations to contact for additional information.

A perfect resource for both students and the general reader, Greenhaven's Contemporary Issues Companion series is sure to be a valued source of current, readable information on social problems that interest young adults. It is the editors' hope that readers will find the Contemporary Issues Companion series useful as a starting point to formulate their own opinions about and answers to the complex issues of the present day.

Introduction

In February of 2007 Stacy Armour and Dana Haynie, sociologists at Ohio State University, published a paper in the *Journal of Youth and Adolescence* demonstrating that the earlier teens begin having sex, the more likely they are to become delinquents. Armour and Haynie came to this conclusion by sorting through data from the National Longitudinal Study of Adolescent Health—the only nationally representative study of adolescent sexuality ever conducted, spanning eight years and surveying more than 90,000 U.S. teens. The Ohio State researchers looked at a sample comprised of 7,000 adolescents. They calculated the "average age of sexual debut" for each student's geographical area, and then broke the teens into three groups: those that started having sex at the locally normal age, those that started early, and those that started later than the norm. Armour and Haynie found that the early starters were also more likely to engage in deviant behavior such as shoplifting, vandalism, and drug-dealing. They concluded that there was a causal link between early sexual debut and long-term delinquency: "The timing of events such as sexual activity," Armour wrote, "can have profound consequences for adolescents, particularly when they occur prematurely."

Armour's and Haynie's research received almost no coverage in the press, as it confirmed well-established conventional wisdom: Most health education programs already teach that teenage sexual activity leads to behavioral problems, substance abuse, and depression.

Nonetheless, these results troubled a group of psychologists at the University of Virginia. These researchers suspected that sex did not cause delinquency, but rather that the two had a related genetic under-pinning. This team, led by Kathryn Paige Harden, took the same sample of 7,000 teens, and narrowed it to a group of 500 same-sex twins (both identical and fraternal)—i.e., sets of adolescents that share the same (or highly similar) genetic material, home life, and school/social environments. Harden's team then looked at sets of twins in which one twin had an earlier sexual debut. If Armour's and Haynie's analysis was accurate, then the "earlier" twins should be more delinquent than the "normal" or "late" twins. Harden's team found no such correlation—and, in fact, found that the "earlier" twin was *less* likely to develop disconcerting behavioral problems. Furthermore, Harden's study found that the identical twins were much more likely to have the same age of sexual debut than the fraternal twins, which would support the supposition that there is a genetic factor determining how early one begins having sex, just as there is an established genetic influence on delinquent behaviors (a hypothesis already supported by several studies). Harden's report—published in the March 2008 issue of the *Journal of Youth and Adolescence*—cites a few other papers that find benefits associated with earlier sexual debut, such as a small German study demonstrating that some women who lost their virginity earlier ultimately showed less intense physical reactions to, and quicker recovery from, stress.

Although Harden's study made no claims as to *why* earlier sexual debut was linked to lower rates of delinquency, she cautiously noted "our hypothesis as a result of this finding is that teens who become involved in intimate romantic relationships early are having sex early and more often, but that those intimate relationships might later protect them from becoming involved in delinquent acts." According to Harden, her work "really calls into question the usefulness of abstinence education for preventing behavior problems . . . and questions the bigger underlying assumption that all adolescent sex is always bad."

This idea that sex is, in and of itself, harmful to minors is relatively new. Judith Levine, author of *Harmful to Minors: The Perils of Protecting Children from Sex*, notes that although "in the professional literature, sex among young people is referred to as a 'risk factor,' along with binge drinking and gun play . . .", this conviction that sex "poses an almost existential peril to children, that it robs them of their very childhood, was born only about 150 years ago," with the advent of psychoanalysis.

Prior to this development, there was no clearly codified idea that a stormy intermediate state between childhood and adulthood existed. In many cultures the onset of puberty—which, in past centuries, was also somewhat later, at around 17 years old for boys and 15 for girls—ushered one into adult responsibilities in the community. The term "adolescence," as we use it today, was coined in the late 1800s by pioneering American psychologist G. Stanley Hall. Hall is remembered for his research in childhood development and is considered the founder of adolescent psychology. In his landmark work, *Adolescence: Its Psychology and Its Relations Anthropology, Sociology, Sex, Crime, Religion and Education,* Hall identified adolescence as a universally experienced period of "Storm and Stress," chiefly characterized by conflicts with parents, extreme moodiness, and risk taking.

During adolescence, Hall wrote: "new dangers threaten all sides. It is the most critical stage of life, because failure . . . almost always means retrogression, degeneracy, or fall." Hall identified sexual desire as the greatest threat in this stressful, stormy progress toward adulthood.

Fortunately, current research indicates that, although a significant minority of teens endure a "stormy" adolescence, this is by no means a universal experience. Furthermore, it would seem that Harden's research directly contradicts Hall's claim; far from being a catastrophic threat to the orderly passage into adulthood, sex is, for some adolescents, a vital stabilizing force, preventing them from going astray. Sex education in the United States, however, is still based on theories like Hall's, and thus focuses exclusively on risk management, stressing the dangers of any sexual intercourse. While some argue that it is dangerous to insist on discussing adolescent sexuality without taking new research, like Harden's, into account, others maintain that teaching anything other than abstinence is an even bigger threat.

Contemporary Issues Companion: Teens and Sex explores some of the complex issues surrounding contemporary adolescent sexuality. The selections included here give a broad view of the current debates over sex education, mandatory human papillomavirus vaccination, and the realities of teen pregnancy, parenting, abortion, sexually transmitted infections, and gender-identity. In imagining how discussions of adolescent sexuality should evolve, people may recall an observation made by the president and founder of the Children's Defense Fund, Marian Wright Edelman: "The best contraception is a meaningful future."

CHAPTER 1

Controversial Aspects
of Teens and Sex

Contrasting Attitudes Toward Teen Sex in the United States and Europe

Elizabeth Agnvall

Raising children with her Swedish husband, American health journalist Elizabeth Agnvall became curious about the contrasting attitudes toward teen sex held in Western Europe and the United States. She discovered that, although teens in the United States and Western Europe engage in comparable levels of sexual activity, the outcomes are very different: Despite steady declines over the past decade, U.S. rates of teen pregnancy, childbirth, abortion, and sexually transmitted infections continue to be among the highest in the industrialized world. Europeans, she found, accept sex as a normal part of adolescence, and work to communicate clear messages on disease- and pregnancy-prevention without urging abstinence. By contrast, Agnvall noted that teens in the United States are bombarded with contradictory messages and incomplete or biased information on contraception, pregnancy, and sexually transmitted infections. The author concludes that U.S. sex education curriculum often seems to be set to serve a political agenda far removed from any objective assessment of what constitutes healthy development.

In our bicultural household—I am American, my husband is Swedish—we are trying to raise our children with the language, cultures and values of both countries. In most cases this isn't difficult. In one area, however, our values differ widely: My husband, reflecting the predominant view in Sweden and much of Western Europe, thinks sex is a normal part of adolescent development. Like many in this country, I disagree, believing it's better for teens to wait—if not until marriage, at least until they are in an adult, loving relationship.

Elizabeth Agnvall, "Is Teen Sex Bad?" *Washington Post*, May 16, 2006, p. HE01. Reproduced by permission of the author.

As a health journalist, I wondered if one way of thinking is demonstrably healthier, physically and psychologically. I resolved to find out.

Among the findings that surprised me: Although prevalent attitudes on teen sex differ in Western Europe and the United States, the views of leading researchers and doctors on both sides of the Atlantic do not. Their opinions lean much closer to the European model. They tend to agree that the mixed message America sends to teens about sex—authorities say "don't" while mass media screams "What are you waiting for?"—endanger our children.

The outcome? Levels of teen sexual activity look remarkably similar here and abroad, but U.S. *rates* of teen pregnancy, childbirth, abortion and *sexually transmitted* diseases are among the highest of all industrialized nations, despite recent decreases. . . .

Teen Sex Is Considered Normal in Western Europe

Pierre-Andre Michaud, chief of the Multidisciplinary Unit for Adolescent Health at the University of Lausanne Hospital in Switzerland and a leading researcher in European teen sexuality, dismisses the idea—widely held in the United States—that sex constitutes risky behavior for teens. In an editorial in May's *Journal of Adolescent Health*, he wrote:

"In many European countries—Switzerland in particular—sexual intercourse, at least from the age of 15 or 16 years, is considered acceptable and even part of normative adolescent behavior." Switzerland, he noted, has one of the world's lowest rates of abortion and teen pregnancy. Teens there, like those in Sweden and the Netherlands, have easy access to contraceptives, confidential health care and comprehensive sex education.

A 2001 Guttmacher Institute report, drawing on data from 30 countries in Western and Eastern Europe, concluded: "Societal acceptance of sexual activity among young people, combined with comprehensive and balanced information about sexuality and clear expectations about commitment and prevention childbearing and STDs [sexually transmitted diseases] within teenage relationships, are hallmarks of countries with low levels of adolescent pregnancy, childbearing and STDs." The study cited Sweden as the "clearest of the case-study countries in viewing sexuality among young people as natural and good."

Cecilia Ekéus, a nurse midwife with a PhD in public international health who works with the Institute of Women and Child Health at Karolinska Institute in Stockholm, says Swedish society teaches that sex should occur in a committed relationship "and also that teenagers should use contraceptives, be informed and take responsibility. But in general we are open and positive and think that it's okay."

Clear Messages on Presenting STDs and Pregnancy

In Sweden, compulsory sex education starts when children are 10 to 12. Without parental consent, teens can get free medical care, free condoms, prescriptions for inexpensive oral contraceptives and general advice at youth clinics. Emergency contraceptives (the so-called morning-after pill) are available without a prescription.

Religion tends to insert itself less in government policy on sex education, contraception and abortion in Western Europe than in the United States, says Michaud. The Catholic Church exerted minimal influence in Switzerland's AIDS prevention campaign, he said. "All in all, the church has been very tolerant and does not really get involved in sexual matters," Michaud wrote in an e-mail.

Straightforward messages on how to prevent STDs and teen pregnancy help offset the impact on teens of sexually explicit ads, movies and other mass media—as ubiquitous in

Western Europe as in the United States, said Robert Blum, chair of the Department of Population and Family Health at the Johns Hopkins [University] Bloomberg School of Public Health.

Western Europe also attaches more social stigma to teen pregnancy and teen motherhood than do some American subcultures, says Bill Albert, spokesman for the National Campaign to Prevent Teen Pregnancy, a U.S. group: "The focus [in Western Europe] is much more on preventing pregnancy and less on sex itself," Albert said.

Europeans Do Not Urge Abstinence

Although some experts argue that economic, educational and racial diversity in the U.S. distort national figures and invalidate comparisons with more homogenous Western European countries, Michaud said he has studied Swiss teens who have dropped out of high school, used drugs or lived in disadvantaged areas of the country. They tend to use contraception regardless of economic status, he said.

"My feeling is that it is impossible to have a double message toward young people," Michaud said, in a phone interview from his Lausanne office. "You can't say at the same time, 'Be abstinent, it's the only fair, good way, to escape from having HIV . . . and at the same time say,' Look, if you ever happen to have sex, then please do that and that and that.' You probably have to choose the message."

Abstinence, he said, is not something the Swiss press on teens. "We think it's unfair. It's useless. It's inefficient. We have been advocating the use of the condom . . . and I think that we tend to be šuccessful."

Joan-Carles Surís, head of the research group on adolescent medicine at the University of Lausanne, puts it another way:

"The main difference is that in the States sexual activity is considered a risk. Here we consider it a pleasure."

The United States Offers Inconsistent Sex Ed

Of course there is no official U.S. position on teen sex, but a portion of the federal Healthy People 2010 report summarizes a set of carefully balanced goals: reduce unwanted pregnancies; cut the proportion of unmarried teens who have had sex; increase the use of birth control and disease prevention techniques among teens who are sexually active; and make contraception, including emergency contraception, more widely available.

But in practice, teens in our culturally heterogenous American society receive many conflicting messages. Many churches in the United States urge abstinence until marriage. Under government and local citizen pressure, many school sex education programs express disapproval of premarital sex and limit information about contraception. A 1999 Kaiser Family Foundation study found that about a third of U.S. public high schools have sex education programs that advocate strict abstinence until marriage. Experts at the Sexuality Information and Education Council of the United States say the number has since grown, with some states not only accepting federal funds for abstinence education, but also including federal government language in their sex education guidelines.

Mary Stetson is a Fairfax County health and physical education teacher who has taught sex education for 11 years. (State guidelines suggest sex ed should run from kindergarten through 12th grade, but individual school districts can decide whether or not to teach it, and parents can have their kids opt out.) Her course focuses on decision-making and values clarification, with an emphasis on encouraging kids not to have sex until marriage. Students learn the consequences of impulsive and risk-taking behavior. Some of her religiously oriented students take abstinence pledges.

Students' outside-class knowledge of sex tends to vary based on their parents' education and socioeconomic status.

"The more education the parent has, the more likely the parents are going to talk to kids about sex," she said.

Mixed Messages About Sex

Poverty alone (the United States is home to a greater proportion of poor teens than Western Europe) doesn't account for the disparity in teen sex behavior here and abroad. According to a 2001 Guttmacher study, the poorest U.S. teens are nearly 80 percent more likely to have a child by 18 than similar teens in Britain.

Outside the classroom, U.S. teens face a barrage of provocation. A study last month in the journal *Pediatrics* found that the higher the exposure to sexual content in movies, TV, music and magazines, the more likely teens were to have intercourse. The study found "frequent and compelling portraits of sex as fun and risk-free."

This message falls on too many teens who are ill-informed or unprotected, says Robert Blum, chairman of the department of population and family health at the Johns Hopkins Bloomberg School of Public Health. "We have a very hypersexualized media and, concurrent with that, a total aversion to giving clear and consistent messages about how you reduce risk," he says. In a 1995 survey, he asked both teens and their parents if the teens had had sex. Half the parents who said their kids were not sexually experienced were wrong, he said. (According to a 2003 survey by the Centers for Disease Control, nearly half of all U.S. students in grades 9–12 have had sex.)

But many American educators and parents say more permissiveness is not the way to go.

Angela Griffiths, executive director of an abstinence-based sex education program in California called Await & Find, said she sees an attitude among some California educators that teen sex is inevitable. Her program focuses on how condoms and birth control sometimes fail to prevent pregnancy and disease, and on the benefits of postponing sex. She said many educators are unwilling to combat what she called the prevailing media attitude that sex is fine for teens.

Too many teachers "are accepting that this is part of youth," she said.

Twisting Research to Serve Agendas

Jonathan Klein, chairman of the American Academy of Pediatrics Committee on Adolescents, says there is a risk that children's best interests are getting lost in the debate over teen sexuality.

"We have some groups in our country who would like to prevent unintended pregnancy and sexually transmitted diseases, and some groups that would like to prevent people from having sex," Klein said. Both are willing to twist research to support their position, he said.

Regardless of a parent's opinions about teen sex, he said, more open communication is healthier: "Healthy sexual behavior is part of development. From a medical perspective it's important that parents and children and teenagers are well-educated about the implications of normal, psychosocial and sexual development."

But what of the emotional consequences? While a series of decades-old studies tied teen sex to other risky behaviors—like drug and alcohol use—many researchers say those findings are not nationally representative. Newer research has linked teen alcohol and drug use to failure to use a condom and more sexual partners, but there's no proof a cause-and-effect relationship exists, or, if it does, which behavior might trigger the other.

Resistance to Seeing Teen Sex as Positive

"Although advocates of abstinence-only government policy have suggested that psychological harm is a consequence of sexual behavior during adolescence, there are no scientific data suggesting that consensual sex between adolescents is harmful," wrote Columbia University's John Santelli in the January issue of the *Journal of Adolescent Health*. That's despite several studies that have looked at the psychological impact of sex on teens.

Where mental health problems are associated with early sexual activity, he says, research suggests that the sexual activity is a consequence of the psychological problems, not vice versa.

In research recently [as of May 2006] published in the *Journal of Adolescent Health*, Lydia Shrier, an assistant professor of pediatrics at Harvard Medical School and director of clinic-based research for the division of adolescent/young adult medicine at Children's Hospital Boston, showed that sexually active people aged 15 to 21 reported more positive feelings on the days they had sex than on the days they didn't. Shrier said sex education messages should take that into account.

"We have to tailor the messages to reflect our understanding that for many people, sex is not a bad thing or a thing that is ridden with guilt, but as a more positive and less negative experience, for some of these young people, than other things in their lives," Shrier said.

The Major Difference Is Contraception

U.S. and Western European teens start sexual activity at about the same age—the median age for first intercourse is 16 in Sweden, 17 in Switzerland, Germany and the United States, and 18 in France.

Chief of the Multidisciplinary Unit for Adolescent Health at the University of Lausanne Hospital in Switzerland, Pierre-Andre Michaud says Swiss teens differ from their U.S. counterparts principally in that they are more likely to use contraceptives.

Almost half (47 percent) of all U.S. high school students report having had sexual intercourse, according to a 2003 survey conducted for the Centers for Disease Control and Prevention; for high school seniors, the figure is 62 percent. In Sweden approximately 80 percent of teens have had sex by age 20, according to Tanja Tydén, professor in the Department of Public Health and Caring Services at Uppsala University in Sweden.

U.S. Teens Have Sex Earlier, More Casually, and Without Effective Protection

U.S. teens are more likely to have sexual intercourse before age 15 and to become pregnant than teens in England and Wales, France and Sweden, according to a 2000 report from the Guttmacher Institute, a nonprofit group that studies sexual health. The study also found that Western European teens are likelier to be in a committed relationship when they have sex.

U.S. teens also have a higher rate of infection and STDs—due to lower condom use, according to the report.

The U.S. teen pregnancy rate (84 out of every 1,000 girls age 15 to 19 become pregnant each year) is higher than that of Denmark (23), Finland (21), Germany (16) and Sweden (25), found a 2000 report in Family Planning Perspectives. (Differences in birth rates are also striking: Roughly six out of every 1,000 teen girls have babies every year in Switzerland, eight per 1,000 in Sweden, 10 per 1,000 in France, and 28 per 1,000 in England and Wales, according to the report, compared to about 54 per 1,000 in the United States. The U.S. abortion rate (then 29 per 1,000) was higher than that in Sweden (17), France (10), Finland (10) and the Netherlands (4), found the report.

According to the Guttmacher Institute, a third of all U.S. girls become pregnant before they turn 20; 80 percent of them are unmarried.

In the U.S., rates of teen sex, pregnancy, abortion and birth have all declined since 1991, as a result, most experts agree, of a combination of teens' postponing sex and increased contraception. But the rates are still higher than those in virtually all Western European countries.

Abstinence-Only vs. Comprehensive Sex Education

Sharon Lerner

Sharon Lerner is a journalist and a senior fellow at the Center for New York City Affairs at the New School. Between 1998 and 2008 she wrote on a wide variety of issues, especially focusing on women's issues, reproductive politics, and the impact these have on teens. In the following article, she explores the divide created when one Midwestern town—faced with a highly emotional debate over what should be included in their public school health curriculum—divided the health program into two classes, one teaching traditional "comprehensive" sex education (including information on anatomy, pregnancy, sexually transmitted infections, safer sex, and contraception), and the other teaching that "sex outside of wedlock is physically, emotionally, and spiritually dangerous." Lerner asserts that dividing the curriculum inevitably also divided the community—students and adults alike— and left many concerned that more public funding was being poured into teaching children less useful or inaccurate information.

If Maple Grove Senior High chose a prom queen, Ashley Gort would have had a good shot at the crown. Ashley, a petite and popular junior with delicate features, wore deep-sea blue to the event, accessorizing her fully beaded gown with a blue necklace like the one Kate Winslet wore in *Titanic* and matching blue rhinestones scattered over her pale blond hair. Her boyfriend, Mike Conlin, borrowed his uncle's Lexus to ferry Ashley to dinner at Landmark Center in St. Paul, Minnesota. Driving away from the restaurant on an unseasonably warm night a few months ago, the couple looked as if they might be headed off for a romantic evening. But while many of their classmates spent the wee hours in rented hot tubs or boogying in Minneapolis clubs, Ashley and Mike drove the half-hour north to a friend's finished basement in their suburban hometown. With their parents stationed upstairs and peeking in at regular intervals, Ashley, Mike, and a few other couples watched movies, played Ping-Pong, and talked until dawn. They did not drink, smoke, or, as Ashley puts it, "touch each other inappropriately."

"We couldn't get like all close with each other," Ashley explains. Per an agreement they struck with their parents, the kids were allowed to cuddle and hold hands, but physical contact ended there. "Couples weren't allowed in rooms by themselves," says Ashley. "There was nothing else you could do, really."

If such rules sound strange, they don't to Ashley and many of the other kids enrolled in the Osseo School District's abstinence-until-marriage class, which teaches students that sex outside of wedlock is physically, emotionally, and spiritually dangerous, while carefully omitting information about birth control, homosexuality, abortion, and other topics that might muddy the message. The curriculum includes sections on "good touch versus bad touch" and refusal skills, and the *Sexuality, Commitment and Family* textbook features a diagram meant to help students figure out exactly where to draw the line (arrows endorse handholding and talking, but a red danger sign appears at necking).

A Sex-Ed Compromise

While almost a quarter of the nation's school districts now [as of 2001] teach abstinence this way, Osseo schools have earned a page in sex-ed history for offering both of the conflicting approaches to teen sex that have riven the country. Students here can take either the new abstinence class or the traditional course, which both warns kids against sex and prepares them for it with information about condoms and such. For Ashley, the choice was simple: "They talk about gays and lesbians and stuff like that, and I personally don't want to hear about that," she says of the older option. "I want to marry the opposite sex. I want to spend my life with that one person and share things with that one person and not other people."

For Josh Goldberg, a baseball player and good student who is in Ashley's grade at Maple Grove, the sex-ed decision was also a no-brainer. Josh went for the more explicit of the two health courses. Though some students have taken to calling this the "slutty" class, Josh would hardly fit anyone's definition of the term. As a sophomore, he counted himself among his school's "normal people group," which he translated to mean that he and his friends didn't drink or go to parties and "there's a lot of people who are a lot more weird than us." Indeed, when I met Josh on the first of several visits to Maple Grove, he and his friends seemed to be spending most of their free time jumping up and down on a trampoline in the Goldbergs' yard and playing with walkie-talkies. ("Come in, Josh. Come in, Josh. You're going to fail your driving test." Hysterical laughter.) Still, when it was time to sign up for health—a requirement for graduation—Josh and most of his friends opted for what he calls the "regular class," while most of Ashley's friends joined her in taking the abstinence-until-marriage course.

And so it is with students in Osseo's three senior-high and four junior-high schools: Kids who share Bunsen burners and school colors and class presidents split into two camps to hear two seemingly irreconcilable perspectives on sex. This sorting clearly has something to do with the students' own feelings about sex. (Of her few friends who didn't take abstinence class, Ashley worries, "Gosh, I would have thought they would've liked to be in this class.") But the division has even more to do with their parents. Between the two classes and the two adult factions still fighting bitterly over what should go on in the classes, it can sometimes seem as if the national fault line over sex education runs right through Osseo, Minnesota.

Parents Battle Over Curriculum

It was a snowy morning six years ago when Ashley's mother, Jeri Gort, felt the first rumblings of Osseo's war over sex ed. The day started out like any other in the Gort house; Jeri kissed her husband, Randy, good-bye as he headed off to work, wrangled Ashley and her younger sister through breakfast, and then bundled up her daughters and headed out toward the bus stop. When she got there, another mother mentioned that Ashley's fifth-grade teacher would define sexual intercourse in class that year—and everything shifted for Gort. "At that moment, I truly believe the Holy Spirit came down and made me teary and gave me the grieving of the heart," she marveled recently [as of 2001]. Standing on the corner, watching her daughters and their friends run around in the snow, the innocence of all of Osseo's children suddenly weighed on her. "I knew then that things needed to change."

That Jeri Gort would be the one to change things in Osseo was also, as she sees it, a matter of divine intervention. "Most Christian women are soft, but I'm not soft and I'm not sweet. I'm an oddity," she said recently, as if she were explaining the fact of her blue eyes or her Minnesota-blond hair. "God made me a little rough around the edges. That's why He spoke to me that day."

As she stands just five feet tall in white canvas sneakers, with a gentle, Midwestern voice, Gort's rough edges aren't immediately apparent. Still, she is the one most people around here credit—or blame, depending on their point of view—for first stoking tensions over the Osseo schools' approach to sex and then pushing through the district's Solomonic attempt to resolve them. Starting from that simple bus-stop revelation,

Gort managed to create an abstinence class in a school district where most parents didn't see the need for one and thus set up a road map for conservatives around the country who wanted to do the same.

After hearing about the imminent lesson, Gort decided to "opt" Ashley out of, taking her to lunch on definition day rather than having her exposed to the information. Shortly after, she took herself down to the Osseo District office to review all the sex-education materials and began speaking at parents' meetings about what she saw there. Not only did sex come up earlier than she would have liked, she reported to parents throughout the district, but the subject was introduced before marriage was. Perhaps most troubling to Gort were the descriptions of different methods of contraception, which she took as an invitation for kids to have sex. "Only half of high-school kids have sex," she told one group, citing the figure that has become the half-empty glass of sex-education debates. "What about the kids who don't have sex? What about supporting them?"

Josh Goldberg's mother, Tobe, one of the parents assembled at that meeting in the Maple Grove Elementary School library, was more concerned with preventing disease and pregnancy in the half of kids who inevitably will have sex. "You can't have too much information," the mother of two is fond of saying. "That woman wants to get rid of sex ed," is what she actually whispered to her husband Arlin that night as they sat squeezed into the child-size chairs in the library. The Goldbergs had already had "the talk" with Josh and his then-10-year-old brother, Noah, making sure that they knew the basics of reproduction and why it's so important to put it off until later. But Goldberg also wanted her boys to hear about both sex and birth control at school. So when Gort said she was starting a group to reconsider the sex-ed program, Goldberg joined.

Officially, Osseo's Human Sexuality Curriculum Advisory Committee was just supposed to make recommendations to the school board about how to update sex-education material. In practice, though, monthly meetings were both more intimate and more explosive than that, with Gort leading the committee majority and Goldberg serving as the spokesperson for the much smaller faction that wanted to keep sex ed as it was. The two sides were able to agree on a few things—that pictures of animals with their babies were appropriate for the younger children, for instance, and that fifth-graders were ready to learn about the physical changes that happen in puberty. But on most other issues, people who might have otherwise been exchanging niceties in the supermarket ended up attacking one another's views on the most personal of questions: Did the clitoris deserve mention in a discussion of female anatomy? Did children need to learn about masturbation? Homosexuality?

Gort suggested that the subject of abortion, which was introduced in eighth grade along with sexual orientation and masturbation, offended some parents and should be removed. In response, another mother muttered something about returning to back-alley days, slammed her eighth-grade textbook shut, and—as others in the dwindling Goldberg camp had already done—stomped out of the sexuality-committee room for good. Committee members also spent months arguing over birth control and the nature of pornography.

A Cultural and Religious Divide

As the debate became more specific (several meetings were devoted entirely to the failure rates of condoms), their positions reflected a more fundamental divide. You could see it as political—Goldberg, who eventually became the only person in her camp, was also the only self-described liberal among about two dozen committee regulars. Or you could see the district's struggle as part of its booming development. The 66-

square-mile patch that makes up the Osseo School District used to be potato country, but in the past 20 years, while the number of students in the district has doubled, the area has morphed into the kind of tidy suburb that so many Americans now call home. And as curlicues of manicured streets have unfurled and Babies "R" Us, Barnes and Noble, and Starbucks have sprung into service, some have mourned for Osseo's rural past. Sexuality-committee chairman Dean Potts seemed nostalgic both for Osseo's roots and for his own boyhood on a North Dakota farm, where he learned both his conservative values and a certain frankness about sex. ("At grade level four or five, I was personally out pulling lambs out of ewes," Potts recalled fondly.)

The religious split was even plainer. One of a handful of Jews in Maple Grove and the only Jew on the committee, Tobe Goldberg reached an icy standoff with Potts, who was studying to be a minister in the Church of the Nazarene throughout his tenure as chairman. Another committee member, Tony Hoffman, quoted Scripture when he argued against an educational video that he felt wrongly portrayed gay men with AIDS as victims. And while Goldberg stopped even exchanging pleasantries with her fellow members, a core group of mothers Gort calls the "prayer warriors" was gathering regularly at her house to pray. The prayer warriors prayed for the success of the abstinence class in their cars, while walking, or sometimes even in the hallways and parking lots outside important sexuality-committee meetings.

The prayer warriors were also there when the school board formalized these ideological differences three years ago [1998]. Jeri Gort talks of the plan that the board approved by a 3-2 vote as a compromise. But Tobe Goldberg didn't experience it that way. Not only did the school board create the new two-track health program over her objections; it also approved the committee's proposal to change the definition of sex that all students would hear. After that board meeting, which stretched until 3 A.M., sexual intercourse was officially no longer an act between any two people but one that occurs between married parents of opposite sex "when the father's erect penis is inserted into the mother's vagina."

In the Abstinence Classroom

On the wall of sex-ed instructor Chris Meisch's classroom there is a saying spelled out in orange and black construction paper: "No knowledge is more crucial than that of health." Tacked up nearby are posters addressing why it's important not to drink and drive and why tobacco is so dangerous. On the first day of the family-life section of Meisch's third-period abstinence-until-marriage class, there is also a question on the board: "What is love?" Students filtering in after the 9:37 bell obligingly search for an answer. "The feeling you have for people in your family?" one boy asks hopefully. "When you care about someone a lot, even more than you can say?" offers another. When no one comes up with the definition he's looking for, Meisch, a young, athletic-looking teacher, prompts the 10th and 11th graders, asking them to name different kinds of love. By the time they work their way to "boyfriend-girlfriend love"—past love for parents, pets, and chocolate milk—the point is getting clearer: Love doesn't always involve sex. "You fall into infatuation," says Meisch, his tone making it clear that this is not the desired outcome. "You grow into love." A few students jot this down in their notebooks.

The two versions of high-school health impart many of the same lessons: Drugs are bad for you, exercise good, leafy greens essential. But the abstinence-until-marriage version grapples with the more amorphous questions of values in a way that its counterpart does not. The new course takes the long view, explaining that marriage between a man and a woman has been the norm throughout history and that the only safe sex is "with a marriage partner who is having sex only with you." Students hear about what makes a compatible mate and even why they should want to mate in the first place. (Parenting, as one abstinence textbook explains, is "a tremendously rewarding commitment based on responsibility and self-sacrifice.") When the subject of birth control comes up, teachers are supposed to discuss only its failures and emphasize its inadequacy.

Students in abstinence class not only hear this particular take on love and romance, they must also present it. Though Ashley did her oral report on tobacco, others whose presentations involved more controversial topics had to cast them carefully in the negative. So when it came time for her report on teens and sexually transmitted diseases, Carol Christensen steered clear of the "good stuff" about birth control that she says she would have mentioned in the other class, trying instead to make a loopy argument that birth control is bad because of its inconvenience. "Like who's going to go and take out a measuring spoon and measure out the exact spermicide at 1:30 in the morning on a Tuesday night?" she says.

In the interest of preventing such situations, abstinence class offers dating exercises. One homework assignment has students write out their dating standards (extra credit if parents sign them). Another asks, "What do you consider the values of postponing sexual gratification?" Several sections advise on setting limits, though by 10th grade Ashley Gort has figured out many of her own.

The Curriculum Divides the Community

"If I know that a person has had a history, or whatever, then I don't get involved," she explained to me one afternoon as we sat in "Maple Grove Free," a family-oriented evangelical church located near the Dairy Queen here. Though she was then "on hold" with the captain of the basketball team, Ashley had never gone long without a date. The key to such lighthearted socializing was to communicate: "You have to make sure you pick the kind of person who feels the way you do; then it's easier to bring up the subject and everything."

Her mother's guidelines also may have helped. Boys were allowed to come by the house and even hang out with Ashley in the family room. (One time, when she was grounded, three stopped by to pay tribute in a single evening.) But per house rules, the family-room door always remained open. And while Jeri trusted Ashley and the Holy Ghost, whom she credited with giving Ashley the desire to stay pure, she was cheered that her daughter's romances never seemed to last more than a few weeks.

Meanwhile, Josh Goldberg spent his 10th grade more engaged with school and sports than with girls. Still, he felt he had made the right choice about sex ed; abstinence class seemed to leave some teens unprepared. Other students had similar objections to the new class. The *Harbinger*, the Maple Grove High student paper, weighed in with several articles and a searing, unanimous staff editorial condemning the district, the human-sexuality committee, and the school board for "offering a curriculum of questionable value that is as deceptive as it is bigoted." The writers took particular offense over the abstinence textbook, which warned against marrying someone of a different economic, cultural, or religious background. When one mother who supports abstinence confronted the *Harbinger*'s faculty adviser in the school parking lot, tempers flared. She angrily complained that the editorial quoted the abstinence materials out of context, and the adviser, as she tells it, shot back that she was "desperately sad as a fellow Christian that you people have decided to make one of God's greatest gifts such a shameful and divisive thing."

The battle that had already torn up the sexuality committee was spreading. Sam Garst, the father of a senior in the district and the retired CEO of a deer-repellant company, founded Osseo Parents for Straight Talk About Sex and printed a brochure with the headline "How Do You Feel About Spending $96,000 More to Educate Our Kids Less?" (The total cost of new abstinence-education materials and arrangements for splitting up students actually ended up closer to $130,000.) Though he got a few positive responses, Garst also received several phone calls informing him that he was going to hell, dozens of angry e-mails (including one accompanied by a computer virus that wiped out his hard drive), and piles of hate letters. "Hey Sammy," read a typical one. "You go ahead and hand out condoms and pills to your kids, we'll teach ours right and wrong."

Meanwhile, across the ideological divide—and a couple of streets—Garst's neighbor, Scott Brokaw, also felt that he was being attacked for his beliefs. One of two Osseo school board members who championed the new abstinence class, Brokaw says he was wrongly accused of beating his wife by someone who was angry over his position on the sex-ed curriculum. A radio-advertising salesman who calls his opponents "vile and mean-spirited people," Brokaw ended up hiring a lawyer to defend himself against the charge. On another occasion, when Brokaw and his wife were eating in a local restaurant, a table of teachers and parents opposed to the class sent him a drink that, the waitress informed him, was known as a Blow Job.

How Students Choose Sides

For Osseo students, the cost of choosing a side can loom even larger. When he was a junior at Maple Grove High, Andy Caruso went so far as to obtain a waiver of the district's health-class requirement because he feared the assumptions kids might make about his sex life whichever track he chose. "It seems like a personal thing that you don't want all your teachers and your friends to know," he said.

The matter of public perception is, not surprisingly, particularly sticky for girls, who make up the majority of students in Osseo's abstinence-until-marriage classes. Even in a district with female student-body presidents and girls' basketball teams that make it to the state finals, girls are still bound by the "hush-hush" rule, as Jessie Sodren, who took the abstinence-until-marriage class, calls it. According to her then-boyfriend, who took the other class, the opposite is true for boys. "Guys just say, like, 'cool,'" he explains. "They just give each other high fives and stuff."

Another couple who split up for health class is less candid. "I've always known I would save sex for marriage. It's just the way I was brought up," says the girl, a 16-year-old sophomore, whose plans for future include "doing something with money, making it grow and making more money." There would have been no reason to doubt her story had her best friend not mentioned the day before that this same girl had just gone through a terrifying two-and-a-half-month pregnancy scare.

By all student accounts, many sexually active kids end up in the abstinence class—a situation that some attribute to parents who sign them up for it without knowing what's really going on. "I know the kids that were in there and, like, I know some of them shouldn't be in there," explains Josh Goldberg, raising his eyebrows meaningfully. "I don't think their parents have any idea what's going on in their life." Ashley Gort, too, recognizes this. "Some of them, if they do do it, they're probably not even going to marry the guy," she told me, shaking her head.

Indeed, students end up in one class as opposed to the other for all sorts of reasons. Carol Christensen took abstinence because the traditional class conflicted with Spanish. Another student, who identifies herself as a born-again Christian and whose mother got pregnant at 16, signed up for abstinence but landed in the traditional class as the result of an administrative error. And one sophomore says she took abstinence because she heard it was easier than the alternative. When I asked her what she hoped to get out of it, she replied, "a C."

But even kids with the clearest of intentions can't know what's in store for them. For Ashley, the surprise came in the form of Mike, the handsome senior with three jobs who, for the past 10 months, has replaced all her other admirers. With a cell phone and her grandfather's hulking old Cadillac now at her disposal, Ashley can see Mike whenever she's not doing homework, working at Old Navy, or at dance-line practice.

The Gorts do have a few hard-and-fast rules though: If Ashley doesn't check in, she loses the car; her weekend curfew is midnight, no exceptions; and when she comes in, she has to kiss her mother goodnight.

"I have a good nose—I can smell pot from a mile away," says Jeri Gort, who is not above sniffing during this tenderest of evening rituals. "I tell her and her friends, if you start drinking, there's no way you can be a virgin when you graduate." Even with all the work she's done to make sure that her daughter gets the right messages, it still comes down to guarding and worrying for Gort.

The Goldbergs, too, are nervously watching a new relationship blossom. Josh's girlfriend Janessa first started jumping on the trampoline along with Josh and his friends at the end of sophomore year. Next came cuddling on the couch, long phone calls that Josh sometimes conducted under a blanket if his parents were around, and his crash course in rose buying.

Even though they have already had "the talk," the Goldbergs find themselves venturing back into that uncomfortable territory lately, reminding Josh about the girl across the street who got pregnant at 16. They're hoping that their message, along with the instruction he's gotten in school, will protect their son from all that could go wrong on his way to adulthood.

It's not terribly different from what's going on just five minutes away at the Gorts' house.

The Benefits of Abstinence-Only Education

Bridget Maher

Bridget Maher is an analyst on marriage and family issues for the Family Research Council, a conservative Christian nonprofit think tank and lobbying group that "champions marriage and family as the foundation of civilization, the seedbed of virtue, and the wellspring of society." The following report on abstinence and abstinence-until-marriage education, published by the Family Research Council, cites the many costs of teen promiscuity and argues that abstinence is "the only 100 percent effective way to prevent out-of-wedlock pregnancy and STDs." According to Maher, abstinence-focused sex education programs are responsible for recent increases in teens postponing first sexual activity and declines in teen pregnancy and sexually transmitted infection rates. She urges that more public funds be invested in these programs. The report also includes a brief description of four federally funded abstinence-until-marriage programs.

The mainstream media constantly bombards young people with sexually explicit messages. Television programs regularly feature premarital sex and sexually provocative content, giving the impression that all young people are sexually active before marriage. The good news is that despite the media's targeting of young audiences with sex-saturated shows, teens prefer the abstinence message.

Increasing numbers of young people are practicing abstinence today. According to the Centers for Disease Control, the percentage of teens who have had premarital sex declined dur-

Bridget Maher, "Why Wait: The Benefits of Abstinence Until Marriage," *Family Research Council*, February 1, 2007. Reproduced by permission of *Family Research Council*, 801 G Street, NW, Washington, DC 20001, 1-800-225-4008, www.frc.org. The name and logo of *Family Research Council*, and the name and logo of *Washington Watch* and *Family Policy* are registered and protected names and trade or service marks.

ing the 1990s. In 1991, 54 percent of teens said they had had sex, compared to 47 percent in 2003. The decline was particularly notable among teen boys. In 1991, 57 percent of high school boys said they had had sex, compared to 48 percent in 2003.

The fact that more teens are practicing abstinence is no surprise, since most teens view abstinence favorably. Almost all teens (94 percent) believe that teens should be given a strong message from society to abstain from sex until at least after high school. Also, nearly 70 percent of teens said it is not OK for high school teens to have sex, and two-thirds of all sexually experienced teens said they wished they had waited longer to become sexually active. Moreover, most teens think highly of virginity. In 2003, 73 percent of teens surveyed said they are not embarrassed to admit they are virgins.

Abstinence and the Decline in AIDS and Teen Pregnancy

Two studies indicate that abstinence has contributed to the decline in unwed teen birthrates, which declined 24 percent between 1994 and 2003 in the United States. A 2003 study found that the increase in the number of abstinent teens accounted for most of the decline in unwed teen births and 67 percent of the decline in out-of-wedlock teen pregnancies from 1991 to 1995. A recent study conducted by the Centers for Disease Control found that both abstinence and contraception contributed to the decline in teen pregnancy rates between 1991 and 2001. The study attributes 53 percent of the decline in teen pregnancy rates among 15- to 17-year-olds to abstinence and 47 percent to contraceptive use.

Both abstinence and monogamy helped to curb the spread of AIDS in Uganda, where HIV infections reached epidemic proportions in the 1980s. The prevalence of HIV began to decline in the late 1980s and continued throughout the

1990s. In fact, between 1991 and 2000, HIV infection rates declined from 21 percent to 6 percent.

How did this happen? Shortly after he came into office in 1986, President Museveni of Uganda spearheaded a mass education campaign promoting a three-pronged AIDS prevention message: abstinence from sexual activity until marriage; monogamy within marriage; and condoms as a last resort. The message became commonly known as ABC: Abstain, Be faithful, and use Condoms if A and B fail.

The government used a multi-sector approach to spread its AIDS prevention message: it developed strong relationships with government, community and religious leaders who worked with the grassroots to teach ABC. Schools incorporated the ABC message into curricula, while faith-based communities, including Christians, Muslims, and Jews, trained leaders and community workers in ABC. The government also launched an aggressive media campaign using print, billboards, radio, and television to promote abstinence and monogamy.

Condoms were definitely not the main element of the AIDS prevention message. President Museveni said, "We are being told that only a thin piece of rubber stands between us and the death of our Continent . . . they (condoms) cannot become the main means of stemming the tide of AIDS." He emphasized that condoms should be used, "if you cannot manage A and B . . . as a fallback position, as a means of last resort."

Several reports show that the decline in AIDS prevalence in Uganda was due to monogamy and abstinence and not to condoms. According to Dr. Edward Green, an anthropologist at Harvard University and an expert on Uganda's AIDS programs, fidelity to one's partner was the most important factor in Uganda's success, followed by abstinence. A 2004 *Science* study concluded that abstinence among young people and monogamy, rather than condom use, contributed to the decline of AIDS in Uganda.

Negative Consequences of Unwed Teen Sex

Practicing abstinence helps couples to avoid the long-lasting negative consequences of premarital sex, including out-of-wedlock childbearing, sexually transmitted diseases (STDs), emotional problems, promiscuity, and future marital breakup.

Today in the United States, 35 percent of all births are out-of-wedlock. Teen birthrates have declined since the early 1990s, but the highest unwed birthrates are among 20–24 year-olds, followed by those between ages 25–29.

Out-of-wedlock childbearing has negative consequences for parents, children, and society. Unwed mothers and fathers are less likely to marry and more likely to suffer from depression and to live in poverty than are those who do not have children outside of marriage. Children born to teen mothers are more likely than other children to have lower grades, to drop out of high school, to be abused or neglected, to have a child as an unmarried teenager, and to be delinquent. Teen childbearing costs U.S. taxpayers an estimated $7 billion each year for increased welfare, food stamps, medical care, incarceration and foster care costs, as well as lost tax revenue due to government dependency. The gross annual cost to society of unwed childbearing and its negative consequences is $29 billion, which includes the administration of welfare and foster care programs, the building and maintenance of additional prisons, as well as lower education and reduced productivity among unwed parents.

Sexually Transmitted Diseases, Promiscuity, and Divorce

Aside from the risk of pregnancy, those who engage in premarital sex have a high risk of contracting an STD. Each year there are 15 million new cases in the U.S., and more than 65 million people in the U.S. currently have an incurable STD. The most common STD is the human papillomavirus (HPV), an incurable virus that can cause genital warts and is present in nearly all (99.7 percent) cervical cancers. In 1998, nearly 30,000 people died from a sexually transmitted disease or its effects; cervical cancer and HIV were the leading causes of sexual behavior-related death among women while HIV was the single leading cause of such deaths among men.

Each year 3 million teens are infected with an STD, and two-thirds of all new STD infections occur among young people under age 25. Gonorrhea and chlamydia are two of the most common curable STDs among sexually active young people. But both of these STDs can cause pelvic inflammatory disease, which may lead to infertility. Gonorrhea rates are highest among 15- to 19-year-old females and 20- to 24-year-old males; forty-six percent of all reported chlamydia infections occur among girls age 15–19, while 33 percent occur among 20- to 24-year-old women. In 2000, the total direct medical cost for diagnosing and treating nine million new cases of STDs among young people age 15–24 was $6.5 billion, with HIV and HPV accounting for 90 percent of the total cost.

Along with being at risk for STDs, young people who engage in unwed sex are likely to experience negative emotional consequences. A 2005 study of youth in grades 7–11 found that engaging in premarital sex often leads to depression. Compared to girls who abstain, girls who engage in premarital sex are two to three times more likely to be depressed one year later. Teens who engage in premarital sex are also likely to experience regret, guilt, lowered self-respect, fear of commitment and fears about pregnancy and STDs. In addition, they are more likely to commit suicide.

Early premarital sex is also likely to lead to promiscuity and future marital breakup. A 2002 study of over 1,000 sexually experienced high school students found that among those who had sex before age 15, females were more than five times as likely, and males were 11 times more likely to have multiple sexual partners than were those who delayed having sex. Another recent [as of 2006] study found that women who have premarital sex, cohabit or bear children out of wedlock are at higher risk for divorce than women who do not.

The birth control pill provides no protection against STDs. The "typical use" of the pill has an 8 percent failure rate with regard to preventing pregnancy. Condoms are also not 100 percent effective in preventing pregnancy—they have a 15 percent failure rate for "typical use"—and provide only limited protection against STDs. According to a NIH [National Institutes of Health] study, when used consistently and correctly, condoms reduce the risk of gonorrhea in men and provide an 85 percent reduction in HIV/AIDS transmission between men and women. However, this study found no evidence that condoms help to prevent six other STDs, including HPV, chlamydia, genital herpes, and syphilis. In addition, young people often do not use condoms properly. A 2005 study of 509 adolescent girls found that only 35 percent used condoms consistently and only 16 percent used condoms consistently and correctly.

Parental Influence on Teen Sex

Many factors influence a teen's decision on whether or not to have premarital sex, and parents play a major role in this area. In a 2003 poll, 45 percent of teenagers said their parents influenced their decisions about sex most strongly. One way parents affect teens' sexual decision-making is by their marital status. A 2002 study found that adolescents living with a divorced single parent or a remarried parent were more likely to engage in premarital sex than were those living in an intact family.

Parental supervision also plays a big role in whether or not teens engage in sexual activity. A study of over 2,000 public high school students found that the more time youths spent unsupervised, the more likely they were to have had sex. Also, the more time boys were left unsupervised, the higher number of lifetime sexual partners they were likely to have. Among those who had had sexual intercourse, "91 percent said that their last time had been in a home setting, including their own home (37 percent), their partner's home (43 percent), and a friend's home (12 percent), usually after school."

Emotional connectedness between parents and teens and parental attitudes toward sex also greatly affect teen sexual behavior. The Adolescent Health Study found that "high levels of mother-child connectedness are independently related to delays in first sexual intercourse among 8th and 9th grade boys and girls and among 10th and 11th grade boys." A 2005 study found that compared to their peers, teens who perceived that their parents strongly disapproved of sex during adolescence were less likely to have an STD six years later.

The Media, Religion, and Other Influences

The media greatly influences teens' sexual behavior. A study in *Pediatrics* found that teens who watched high amounts of television with sexual content were twice as likely as those who watched minimal amounts to initiate sexual intercourse during the following year. High exposure to sexual content was also associated with advanced forms of non-coital behavior. According to the study, discussions of sex on television had the same effect on teens as depictions of sexual activity.

Religion plays an important role in helping teens to delay premarital sex. In a 2004 report by the National Center for Health Statistics, teens stated that the main reason they had not had sex yet was that it was "against their religion or morals." A 2003 study found that teens, particularly girls, who pray, believe religion is important, attend church regularly, and participate in youth groups are less likely to have pre-marital sex than are less religious teens.

Drug and alcohol use, as well as delinquency, are associated with premarital sex. Teens who drink are seven times more likely, and those who use drugs are five times more likely to have sex than those who do not. Also, sexually experienced teens are likely to use substances such as alcohol and cigarettes. In a 2002 survey, almost one-third of sexually active young people age 15–24 said they had "done more" sexually than they had planned while drinking or using drugs.

According to a Department of Justice report, boys who engage in delinquency at an early age are likely to become teen fathers, and teen fathers are likely to engage in delinquent behavior. The report found that compared to teens who were not fathers, teen fathers were 7.5 times more likely to engage in serious delinquency during the same year they became fathers.

Comprehensive Sex-Ed Programs

Young people are also very much affected by the messages on sex and abstinence that they receive in school. Unfortunately, the majority of schools teach "safe sex" or "comprehensive sex ed" programs which encourage contraceptive use and assume that young people will engage in sexual activity. Some experts claim that abstinence programs and comprehensive sex ed programs are becoming more similar. However, this is not the case. The underlying message of comprehensive sex ed programs is that sexual activity is OK for teens as long as they use "protection." According to a 2002 report conducted by the Physicians Consortium, which investigated comprehensive sex programs promoted by the Centers for Disease Control, abstinence is barely mentioned and condom use is clearly advocated in these curriculums. Not only do students learn how to obtain condoms, but they also practice putting them on cu-

cumbers or penile models. Masturbation, body massages, bathing together, and fantasizing are listed as "ways to be close" in one curriculum.

The Sexuality Information and Education Council of the United States (SIECUS) developed guidelines for comprehensive sex education, which according to SIECUS have become "one of the most influential publications in the field." These guidelines call for teaching five- through eight-year-olds about masturbation, sexual intercourse, accepting cohabitation, and homosexuality. Upper elementary students learn about these topics as well as contraception and abortion. Topics for junior high students include sexual fantasies, body massages, and oral, vaginal, and anal intercourse. For high school students, SIECUS recommends adding discussion about using "erotic photographs" [otherwise known as pornography] and literature. Only one page out of one hundred is dedicated to abstinence.

Abstinence-Until-Marriage Programs

Parents overwhelmingly reject the messages of comprehensive sex-ed and approve of abstinence education. In a 2004 Zogby poll, only 7 percent of parents approved of teaching teens that it's OK for them to have sex as long as they use condoms to protect against pregnancy and disease. However, 96 percent of parents said that sex-ed classes should teach that abstinence from sexual activity is best for teens. Also, 91 percent of parents said teens should be taught that the best choice is for sexual activity to be linked to love, intimacy and commitment—qualities most likely to occur in a faithful marriage.

Today, there are over one thousand abstinence-until-marriage programs around the United States, and one-third of public middle and high schools both say that abstinence is "the main message in their sex education" and that abstinence is taught as "the only option for young people." In these programs, abstinence is defined as refraining from all sexual activity, including mutual masturbation, genital sexual intercourse, and anal and oral sex. Started by non-profit and faith-based groups, these programs teach young people that abstaining from premarital sex is the expected standard and that "personal happiness, love and intimacy are most likely to occur within the commitment of a faithful marriage." Abstinence programs address youth who have already been sexually active, encouraging them to practice secondary virginity. Also, abstinence curricula teach that human sexuality is "not primarily physical, but moral, emotional, and psychological in nature." Abstinence programs do more than just tell teens to say "No" to unwed sex: They give young people the encouragement and skills they need to practice abstinence. Classes cover many topics, including self-esteem building, self-control, decision making, goal setting, character education, relationship skills, refusal skills, healthy personal and sexual boundaries, emotional and physical consequences of premarital sexual activity, and understanding sexual intimacy and human bonding. The effectiveness of birth control may be discussed, but it is neither provided nor promoted in these programs.

Some people claim that abstinence education is ineffective and presents medically inaccurate information. Rep. Henry Waxman (D-CA), a longtime enemy of abstinence education, makes this claim in a paper commonly known as "The Waxman Report." The report accuses abstinence programs of creating gender stereotypes and of teaching inaccurate information about contraceptives, abortion, and human reproduction. However, almost all of the "scientific errors" he found were not actually errors. They were medically accurate facts that his report took out of context or distorted.

There is plenty of evidence demonstrating the effectiveness of abstinence education. Several studies published in peer-reviewed journals have found that students participating in abstinence programs are more likely to delay sex, to view abstinence more positively and to have an increased knowledge of the negative consequences of premarital sexual activity.

Federal Study on Abstinence Education

An interim report from a federal longitudinal study on four Title V abstinence programs found that abstinence education is effective in changing young people's attitudes with regard to sexual behavior. Compared to their peers in a control group, teens who participated in abstinence programs had an increased understanding of the negative consequences of unwed sex. Also, the students viewed abstinence more favorably and unwed sex more negatively.

Choosing the Best. Choosing the Best [CTB], an abstinence program based in Atlanta, Georgia, has developed curricula and parental education materials that are used nationwide. Since the company started in 1993, over one million students have completed CTB. Students in public or private schools are taught the program by their teachers, who can be trained by CTB staff. CTB has four age-appropriate programs for 6th through 12th graders. Each curriculum teaches students the consequences of premarital sex, the benefits of abstaining until marriage, relationship education, how to make a virginity pledge, refusal skills, and character education. Choosing the Best involves parents in their children's lessons and educates them about how to teach abstinence to their children.

An independent study conducted between 2002–2004 found positive results among students who participated in classes using the Choosing the Best curriculum. The study was based on 7th, 8th, and 9th grade students in a south metro Atlanta high school and its feeder middle school. Students were taught either CTB or the state-approved abstinence program. All students received a pre-test and two post-tests, one immediately following the program and another one twelve months later. Data on 318 students indicated that CTB students were 47 percent less likely to initiate sexual activity.

This abstinence program has also contributed to lower teen-pregnancy rates in Georgia. In Columbus, Georgia, CTB materials were used in all 8th grades for a period of four years. A study requested by the Georgia State Board of Education to examine the effectiveness of this curriculum found a 38-percent reduction in pregnancies among middle-school students in Muscogee County between 1997 and 1999. Other large school districts that did not implement the Choosing the Best program experienced only a 6-percent reduction in teen pregnancies during those same years.

Not Me, Not Now. Not Me, Not Now, a Rochester, New York–based abstinence program, used a local mass media campaign, a user-friendly website, and a school-based program to promote the abstinence message. Television and radio ads, educational materials for parents, posters (and guides to accompany them) for schools, community centers and pediatricians' offices were part of this program, which aimed at youth age 9–14. Postponing Sexual Involvement, an educational series, was used in some elementary and middle schools in Monroe County.

An evaluation conducted between 1994 (before the program started) and 1997 found several positive results. Before the program, 34 percent of the students said they could adequately handle the consequences of sexual activity, compared to 22 percent after the program. Results of the Centers for Disease Control's Youth Risk Behavior Survey for Monroe County (for 1992, 1995 and 1997) found that the percentage of youth having sex by age 15 declined from 46 percent to 32 percent. Also, pregnancy rates among 15- to 17-year-old girls in Monroe County declined 22 percent between 1993 and 1996.

Best Friends. The Best Friends program, founded in Washington, D.C., in 1987 and operating in more than 100 schools in the United States, teaches students about many topics, including friendship, love and dating, self-respect, decision making, alcohol and drug abuse, physical fitness and nutrition, AIDS, and STDs. In addition, the program uses role model presentations, mentoring, community service, and a recognition ceremony at local schools to help young girls abstain from premarital sex, drugs, alcohol and smoking. The Diamond Girls program for high school students focuses on career development and leadership activities during monthly and weekend meetings. A recent study found that the Best Friends program is very effective in preventing junior high and high school girls from engaging in premarital sex or drug or alcohol use. The study compared data on Best Friends girls in grades six through eight in Washington, D.C., with that on District girls the same age who participated in the Centers for Disease Control's Youth Risk Behavior Survey (YRBS). Compared to the YRBS girls, Best Friends girls were more than six times less likely to engage in premarital sex, eight times less likely to use drugs, twice as likely not to smoke and almost twice as likely not to drink alcohol. Researchers controlled for age, grade, and ethnicity or race. Best Friends high school participants, known as Diamond Girls, were also compared to high school girls in the YRBS, both of whom live in Washington, D.C. Compared to YRBS girls, Diamond girls were nearly 120 times less likely to have premarital sex, 26 times less likely to use drugs, nearly nine times less likely to smoke and three times as likely to abstain from alcohol.

Operation Keepsake. Operation Keepsake, a Cleveland, Ohio–based abstinence program started in 1988, teaches its For Keeps curriculum in 90 public and private schools in the greater Cleveland area. It is presently [as of 2006] taught to at least 15,000 middle and high school students. Along with a classroom component, this program also includes peer mentoring, guest speakers, opportunities to make an abstinence pledge, and parental involvement.

A 2005 study on the For Keeps curriculum published in the *American Journal of Health Behavior* found several positive results among 2,069 middle school students, half of whom were taught the For Keeps curriculum. Compared to the control group, students learning For Keeps demonstrated a significant increase in their knowledge of HIV/AIDS and other STDs; a significant increase in their beliefs in being abstinent until married or older; and a decline in their intention to have sex in the near future. Sexually active teens receiving this program reported fewer episodes of sexual intercourse and fewer sexual partners.

Virginity Pledges

Virginity pledges are effective in encouraging teens to delay sexual initiation, but a pledge by itself is not sufficient. Young people also need to participate in an abstinence program and to have family and friends who support and encourage them to remain chaste.

A 2004 study from Columbia and Yale Universities found that teens who make a virginity pledge are 12 times more likely than non-pledgers to be virgins at marriage. Also, those who signed a pledge were more likely to delay sexual activity for 18 months, have fewer partners, and marry earlier. A Heritage Foundation study found that young women who pledge to remain virgins are about 40 percent less likely to have an out-of-wedlock birth compared to those who do not pledge.

Funding for
Abstinence-Until-Marriage Programs

Although funding for abstinence-until-marriage has increased recently [as of 2006], comprehensive sex education and contraception programs are vastly overfunded in comparison. In 2002, abstinence-until-marriage programs received $144.1 million in federal and state government funding, while contraception sex-ed programs received $1.73 billion in 2002. In other words, government spent $12 to promote contraception for every dollar spent on abstinence education. Abstinence-until-marriage programs received about $176.5 million in federal funding in 2006, but there is still a lack of parity between these programs.

Abstinence-until-marriage programs have proven to be very effective in reducing sexual activity among young people. Their success in changing young people's views and behavior is due to the fact that they teach young people that saving sex for marriage is the best choice, one that will benefit them now and in the future. In addition, these programs give students the knowledge and skills they need to abstain until marriage.

Unfortunately, many abstinence organizations lack the financial resources to expand their programs. These organizations are small nonprofits with shoe-string budgets, relying on donations, the sale of their materials, and government funding for survival. Due to their limited resources, they are often unable to meet the demand for their programs. Abstinence programs should receive more funding, because abstinence is the only 100 percent effective way to prevent out-of-wedlock pregnancy and STDs. More funding will enable these programs to bring the abstinence message to more young people, teaching them that the best way to find true happiness, intimacy and love is to save sex for marriage.

The Costs of
Abstinence-Only Education

Heidi Bruggink

Heidi Bruggink is the legal coordinator of the Appignani Humanist Legal Center of the American Humanist Association. The American Humanist Association publishes the Humanist *magazine and is dedicated to applying "Humanism—naturalistic and democratic outlook informed by science, inspired by art, and motivated by compassion—to broad areas of social and personal concern." In the following article, Bruggink argues that abstinence-only education does students a grave disservice: While U.S. teen pregnancy, birth, and abortion rates continue to be among the highest in the industrialized world, more than 80 percent of all abstinence-only programs include "false, misleading, or distorted information about abortion, contraception, and gender roles." Furthermore, Bruggink demonstrates that these programs dangerously intertwine religious and public concerns: Almost one-quarter of the $249 million spent annually by the federal government on abstinence-only education goes to pay for explicitly religious programs, many of which use Christian biblical texts in their teaching materials.*

In Late October 2006 New Jersey became the fourth state to reject federal funding for sex education programs. Thanks to Bush administration mandates, accepting the federal money would have required the state to abandon its existing comprehensive sex-ed curriculum, and instead rely exclusively on abstinence-only programs. But though New Jersey's decision and similar ones by California, Connecticut, and Maine are encouraging, not every state has the luxury of turning down federal dollars. And that's bad news for those concerned about reproductive health.

Heidi Bruggink, "Miseducation: The Lowdown on Abstinence-Only Sex-Ed Programs," The *Humanist*, vol. 67, January-February 2007, pp. 4–6. Copyright 2007 American Humanist Association. Reproduced by permission of the author.

While the U.S. government will spend over $241 million in federal funding on abstinence-only programs in 2007, there's good reason to doubt the effectiveness of the Bush administration's preferred approach. A recent General Accountability Office study concluded that abstinence-only programs suffer from a lack of oversight and found little evidence that they succeed at preventing teen pregnancy. Another study, released in 2004 by Rep. Henry Waxman (D-CA), found that over 80 percent of abstinence-only curricula supported by the Department of Health & Human Services (HHS) contained false, misleading, or distorted information about abortion, contraception, and gender roles, and routinely presented religious beliefs as scientific fact. The results of the Bush administration's promotion of abstinence-only curricula speak for themselves: the nation's teen birth rate, teen pregnancy rate, and abortion rate all remain the highest in the industrialized world.

Cause for Concern

A closer look at the abstinence-only programs that have received federal funding suggests further cause for concern. In 2004 the HHS Capital Compassion Fund announced over $58 million in grants to "grass-roots, faith-based" organizations, including groups like Catholic Charities of Kansas City and Lutheran Family Services of Nebraska. Among the many examples of abstinence-only programs being run with federal dollars by groups with explicitly religious missions is the Silver Ring Thing (SRT). SRT—which urges teens to pledge to refrain from sex until marriage and to make a public show of their commitment by wearing a symbolic silver ring—is the primary outreach of the John Guest Team, whose parent company, the John Guest Evangelistic Team, works, according to its website, "to communicate the message of Jesus Christ to the unchurched through creative, media-based and one-on-one evangelism."

A review of other abstinence-only sex-ed programs only further reinforces the religious undertones being utilized in public schools. The Why kNOw? program directly paraphrases 1 Corinthians 13:4 to describe the true meaning of love: "Real Love is patient; is kind; does not envy; does not boast; is not proud; is not rude; is not self-seeking; is not easily angered; keeps no record of wrongs; does not delight in evil; rejoices with the truth; always protects; always trusts; always hopes; always lasts; [and] never fails." Why kNOw? also quotes the Song of Songs as a "historical book" and states that "though the origin of the name 'French Kissing' is unknown, King Solomon should take credit for the act." The curriculum also places heavy emphasis on studying Judeo-Christian marriage ceremonies and encourages educators to have their middle-school students plan their own weddings, complete with details on which flowers they would use, who would be in their bridal party, and, of course, which (heterosexual, virginal) person they would wed. The program teaches youth that the traditional lifting of the veil shows that "the groom is the only man allowed to 'uncover' the bride" and demonstrates her respect for him by illustrating that she hasn't "allowed any other man to lay claim to her."

Promoting marriage and discouraging premarital sex through fear and false information remains a benchmark of abstinence-only sex education. The Heritage Keepers program repeatedly cites research suggesting that married people have better sex—and many of these statistics are attributed to Glenn T. Stanton, director of global insight for cultural and family renewal and senior analyst of marriage and sexuality at Focus on the Family [a prominent, evangelical Christian organization].

The WAIT (Why Am I Tempted?) Training program also depends heavily on moralistic, pro-marriage information to promote abstinence. The WAIT curriculum includes a game in which students repeatedly place a transparent piece of tape, symbolizing a woman, on a man's arm to show that after several "uses" (sexual acts or partners) the tape is less clean and perfect. Finally, the teacher is instructed to attach the tape to another male volunteer and ask, "If this process gets repeated too many times, do you think it will affect this person's marriage?"

Misleading Curriculum Puts Kids at Risk

Such games aren't unique. Why kNOw? includes a game that compares a stuffed animal named "Speedy the Sperm," which represents a sperm cell, and a penny, used to symbolize HIV. By this reasoning, students are meant to see that if a condom fails 14 percent of the time with something as big as Speedy, it clearly cannot effectively prevent the spread of HIV—which is a thousandth of the size. Despite repeated and conclusive evidence showing that condoms available in the United States don't have holes (if they do, the entire batch is discarded), and that the real reason for error is improper use, not product defect, Why kNOw? continues to teach youth that condoms are useless, apparently believing that this will discourage them from having sex. Predictably, research suggests that young people who believe condoms don't work simply use protection less often—they don't engage in sex at a lesser rate.

Clearly, we do our young people a great disservice by continuing to use such misleading and dangerous curricula. The Bush administration's reliance on abstinence-only sex ed confronts advocates of a more comprehensive (and effective) approach with a strategic challenge: How can we promote healthy sex education without being viewed as morally deficient? Like it or not, many parents remain anxious that comprehensive sex ed takes what they view as one of their most sensitive parenting tasks out of their hands, and puts it into those of teachers and administrators whom they may not trust. Even the most widely effective and highly promoted comprehensive sex-ed programs, such as "Making Proud Choices" and "Draw the Line/Respect the Line;" still include decision-making skills that stress personal choice and limit-setting—topics parents may prefer to teach their children themselves. Public health educators must find a way to maintain or at least respect parental control and personal choice while stressing the need to provide effective factual information to teens.

According to the first-ever global analysis of sexual behavior, married couples have the most sex. And while more people are having sex before marriage, they aren't doing so at increasingly younger ages. The study, conducted by researchers at the London School of Hygiene & Tropical Medicine and published in *The Lancet* on November 2, 2006, gathered data from fifty-nine countries worldwide and concluded that a shift towards later marriage accounts for an increase in premarital sex. Surprisingly, the study showed no correlation between multiple partnerships and higher incidence of sexually transmitted disease; that is, developed nations reported higher rates of multiple partnerships, not those parts of the world which tend to have higher rates of HIV and AIDS, such as African countries. This led the authors to suggest that poverty, immobility, and gender inequality may be a stronger factor in sexual ill-health than promiscuity.

The researchers concluded that no general approach to promoting sexual-health will work everywhere and no single-component intervention is likely to work anywhere. Moreover, public health messages must be guided by epidemiological evidence than by myths and moral stances.

Mandatory HPV Vaccination Is Necessary

Meghan O'Rourke

Meghan O'Rourke is the culture editor for Slate *magazine, poetry editor of* Paris Review, *and an occasional contributor to the* New York Times. *She writes broadly about trends in literature and American culture. In this article for* Slate, *O'Rourke explores the public backlash against Gardasil, a vaccine developed to protect women from infection by the human papillomavirus (HPV) and approved by the United States Food and Drug Administration (FDA) in 2006. Although widespread vaccination against HPV would likely eliminate cervical cancer and reduce the incidence of throat, head, neck, and anal cancers, there is widespread resistance to making HPV vaccination mandatory for schoolchildren. O'Rourke believes that this sentiment has little to do with the efficacy or possible risks of the vaccine: Since Gardasil is administered to pre-adolescents eleven- and twelve-year-old girls, this debate over the vaccine triggers "preexisting latent anxieties about young women and sex." She contrasts this to the vaccination for hepatitis B (also a sexually transmitted disease), which, as it is administered to infants, has not become a disputed territory in the U.S. "war against premarital teen sex."*

In recent months, you may have seen a TV ad featuring striking young women skateboarding and drumming as a voice-over intones, "Every year, thousands of women die from cervical cancer. I want to be one less woman who will battle cancer." The women represented are self-confident, accomplished, artistic, and independent. Only one boy shows up in the ad—in a still photo. But what is most striking about the ad is that it is just one part of a much larger cultural and political battle about young women and sex.

America declared a "war on cancer" 30 years ago, and yet few cures or vaccines have been discovered since. So when [drug company] Merck announced that it had created a drug that could prevent some 70 percent of cervical cancers from developing, you would think Americans would rejoice. Instead, there was a backlash. Last February, Republican Gov. Rick Perry signed an executive order that would have made Texas the first state to mandate the vaccination of schoolgirls against HPV [human papillomavirus], the sexually transmitted virus that is a frequent cause of cervical cancer. He promptly came under fierce attack. The Texas Legislature expressed its deep reservations about the vaccine, and the media reported that Perry had received a campaign contribution from Merck prior to signing the order. Ultimately, the order was vetoed by the legislature. Earlier this year [2007] 24 states were contemplating making Gardasil—as the cervical-cancer vaccine is known—a mandatory vaccination for young women. Today, only one state, Virginia, has such a law, and it leaves a loophole for parents to opt out.

An Illogical Debate

In one sense, this reluctance seems understandable. Merck is the same company that made headlines in 2004 for failing to disclose that its painkiller Vioxx raised the risk of cardiac arrest and stroke in patients. Gardasil is a brand-new drug, and the company has conducted only limited testing on it. Though the pre-release studies suggest it is highly efficacious, the vaccine's long-term side effects are not fully known. What's more, the vaccination comprises three painful shots, at an estimated cost of $360. Given all this, it is hard to blame parents who resist putting their daughters on the drug's front line, preferring to wait until more is known about it.

Much less understandable, though, is the position taken by many opponents: namely, that a cervical-cancer vaccination would "promote promiscuity" among teenage girls. Implicit in this argument is the assumption that good girls don't get cervical cancer; only "loose" ones do—and they may get what they deserve. Earlier this year, State Sen. George Runner of California told the *Los Angeles Times* that American money would be much better spent on other types of vaccines, since cervical cancer is a result of lifestyle choices, rather than bad genetic luck.

This view involves a hefty dose of ignorance, as well as a dollop of old-fashioned magical thinking. As any doctor can tell you, it takes only one sexual contact to contract a strain of HPV that can lead to cervical cancer. The CDC [Centers for Disease Control and Prevention] reports that at least 50 percent of Americans are infected with HPV over the course of their lives, and a whopping 80 percent of American women are infected by age 50. Admittedly, the chances are slim that HPV would lead to cervical cancer: Only a small portion of HPV infections become cancerous. Still, according to the National Cancer Institute, roughly 11,000 women will be diagnosed with cervical cancer this year in the United States. Nearly 3,700 women will die. If you are one of those 3,700 women, you might feel that a vaccine could have changed everything. And—contrary to Runner's insinuations—you needn't be a slut to be among them: You could have married a guy who slept with just one other girl. Or, of course, you could be one of the approximately 13 percent of American women who, according to a 2003 study, are or will be a victim of rape over the course of their lives.

Anxiety About Girls and Sex

Meanwhile, the idea that a mere vaccination could "promote promiscuity" is bizarrely simplistic—as if the prick of a needle in the arm of a pre-adolescent girl stands in for a, well, prick of another kind. For one thing, no evidence suggests a connection between a decrease in HPV and an increase in sexual activity, nor is it likely to: HPV is hardly a major deterrent to kids who might be squeamish about STDs, since it has few short-term effects and cervical cancer usually takes years to develop. Adolescents have a hard enough time thinking about next week, let alone a decade from now. They're more likely to be worried about the immediate effects of herpes, gonorrhea, or syphilis, or even AIDS, which is still more prevalent than cervical cancer. For another thing, there's already a vaccine out there designed to prevent a sexually transmitted disease— and *it's* not being protested by anyone on the grounds that it might encourage promiscuity. That vaccine is for hepatitis B, and it is given to approximately 88 percent of all American children by the time they are 19 months old. Finally, it's not as if adolescents are incredibly rational about their sexual calculations, as the vaccine-promiscuity argument would have Americans believe.

On the contrary, the reason so many legislators and parents have conjured up a tie between vaccination and sex clearly has less to do with objective reality than with the age at which girls are supposed to receive the vaccine. Gov. Perry's executive order would have mandated that girls receive the vaccine as they go into sixth grade, at age 11 or 12—precisely the juncture between childhood and adulthood we're the most uncertain about how to conceptualize. According to [pediatrician] Sydney Spiesel, parents often complain that 11 is too early for a Gardasil shot, because their daughters aren't sexually active yet. But that's not the point; the point is that these pre-adolescents need to receive the vaccine well before they *are* sexually active.

It may be that Merck miscalculated in not finding a way for vaccinations to begin in childhood rather than in pre-adolescence, even if it meant patients needing a booster series. The later age encourages parents and politicians to make a categorical error, associating Gardasil with the pill or with the sex talk, when it needn't be associated at all (just as hep-B shots aren't). Merck may also have miscalculated by recommending that the vaccine be administered only to girls, though boys are carriers of HPV, too—and in fact, scientists believe that the virus plays a role in head and neck cancers as well as anal cancer. Merck is currently testing the drug for boys, but by now the debate has fully catalyzed pre-existing latent anxieties about young women and sex.

The Debate Triggers Psychosomatic Side Effects

Indeed, one of the most fascinating elements of the Gardasil debate is that the hysteria appears to have been internalized by some of the constituents themselves—a twist [father of psychoanalysis, Sigmund] Freud might appreciate. Rumors abound about significant negative side effects, although pre-release statistics show nothing out of the ordinary. (To be sure, early studies may not capture the full range of drug-related risks.) At one school in Australia, 26 girls injected with Gardasil went to the campus medical office complaining of adverse effects; a couple were hospitalized. Since then, additional reports of group dizziness and fainting have been posted in the comments section of various Internet sites. Since many patients now know the vaccine is controversial, one has to wonder whether some of these instances have more to do with sublimated anxiety about sex and with sociogenic effects than with the drug itself. (Spiesel said that none of his patients had reacted adversely, though he had heard of one case where a patient had.)

And so liberal parents who distrust Big Pharma are also highly suspicious of Gardasil. But as Darshak Sanghavi, a pediatric cardiologist, told me, speaking by phone from his office, "Looking at the science, I think it's highly unlikely that there is any significant side effect that hasn't been caught. For sure, there could be something rare. But there is no suggestion of anything masked." He stressed the importance of contextualizing the vaccine, pointing out that it takes a lot of research money to create vaccines, and it is not always a profitable enterprise. Given the very real dangers of cervical cancer, Sanghavi said, "I don't believe that they have pushed [Gardasil] in an unethical manner. They have a product that is almost certainly going to save lives." In the meantime, fears about the health risks of Gardasil have obscured the hidden moral calculus of the conservative opposition to Gardasil: that in the end, it may be worth it for several thousand women to die from cervical cancer every year as collateral damage in the war against premarital teen sex. Because, of course, even if the vaccination *did* encourage promiscuity, it's not clear that it's OK for women to die as a result.

Protesters in all camps of the anti-vaccine coalition are chafing at what they see as the paternalism inherent in making vaccines mandatory. But if anyone in the government is being paternalistically intrusive, it's not the Gov. Perrys of the world. It's the legislators who are pursuing the war against premarital teen sex when they could seize the chance to eradicate the HPV virus and its associated cancers from the lives of young Americans. On second thought, this isn't really paternalistic at all. To pretend for a little longer that their daughters will never grow up, and that we all can protect them by hiding our heads in the sand for another few years—actually, that's just childish.

Mandating the HPV Vaccination Is Premature

Elissa Mendenhall

In this article, Dr. Elissa Mendenhall questions the wisdom of making it mandatory that adolescent girls be vaccinated for human papillomavirus. While both Gardasil and Cervarix—the two available HPV vaccines—seem to be noteworthy medical achievements, Mendenhall is concerned that neither has been extensively, independently tested for safety when used on minors, nor is the long-term efficacy of either vaccines known. Finally, noting that the three-shot Gardasil regimen is priced at $360— making it one of the most expensive vaccines ever brought to market—a universal vaccination program would be prohibitively expensive. Mendenhall also notes that, while these vaccines are nearly 100 percent effective in preventing several strains of HPV responsible for cervical cancer, of those women infected with HPV, only a very small percentage will ever develop cervical cancer, and only a very small portion of those cases will prove fatal. Even with HPV vaccinations readily available, regular gynecological exams and Pap tests continue to be the safest, most effective method of protecting women from cervical cancer. Elissa Mendenhall is a naturopathic physician practicing in the United States.

In September 2006, the State of Michigan approved two measures to require girls entering the sixth grade to be vaccinated with Gardasil, the new vaccine for human papillomavirus (HPV) touted as the "anti-cancer vaccine." Gardasil is widely hailed in the public health community as a giant step toward preventing cervical cancer. After four clinical trials, the

Elissa Mendenhall, "Guard Against Gardasil: As Merck's 'One Less' Campaign Floods the Media, We Ask: Do We Really Know Enough About the New HPV Vaccine to Mandate It for All Preadolescent Girls?" *Mothering*, vol. 142, May-June 2007, pp. 44–49.

FDA [Food and Drug Administration]approved its use in June 2006, and Gardasil is now [as of 2007] available by prescription.

Clinical trials have found that Gardasil is nearly 100 percent effective in preventing certain strains of HPV infection—a tremendous feat in the world of vaccine research. There is no doubt that the introduction of Gardasil has dramatically altered the public-health landscape for both sexually transmitted infections and cervical cancer. But are we ready to make the leap from a handful of promising clinical trials to mandating vaccination for all preadolescent girls?

HPV and Cancer

Humans and HPV have an interesting and complex relationship. HPV is best known for causing common warts and cervical cancer, but there are more than 100 different strains of HPV. Because of the cancer link, the strains that are of the greatest medical concern are those that are sexually transmitted. These strains can cause genital warts, or can be associated with cervical and other cancers of the genital area. Approximately 13 percent of American women are infected with genital HPV. Infection with the HPV virus is an important cofactor in cervical cancer, but very few people infected with HPV will ever get cervical cancer. At least 80 percent of women will have acquired a genital HPV infection by the time they are 50 years old, and about 6.2 million American men and women get a new genital HPV infection each year, according to estimates by the Centers for Disease Control. Compare this to the national rate of cervical cancer. In 2003, the National Cancer Institute estimated the number of cases of cervical cancer at 253,781. In 2002, 4,000 women died from the disease in the US. While this is a sizable number, it represents a tiny fraction of those infected with the virus. HPV infection is asymptomatic in most people. Until recently, most cases went undetected.

With recent advances in detection of the HPV virus, it appears that the norm is more one of infection than of disease. In most cases, the virus's relationship with its host is symbiotic: It causes no harm and is not easily detected. "Although HPV is a necessary cause of cervical cancer, it is not a sufficient cause. Thus, other cofactors are necessary for progression from cervical HPV infection to cancer," states Nubia Munoz in a recent article in the medical journal *Vaccine*. Saying that HPV causes cervical cancer is similar to saying that being of African descent causes sickle-cell anemia: It is an oversimplification that fails to look at other factors. For instance, the World Health Organization notes that up to 30 percent of cervical cancer deaths in the US are attributable to smoking cigarettes.

The Two HPV Vaccines

Two HPV vaccines are currently available or in the works: Gardasil, produced by Merck & Co. and already approved by the FDA; and Cervarix, produced by GlaxoSmithKlein, still awaiting FDA approval [as of late 2007]. Gardasil is a quadrivalent vaccine; that is, it contains four strains of HPV: the two most associated with cervical cancer, and the two most associated with genital warts. The bivalent Cervarix contains the two strains of HPV most associated with cervical cancer. Neither vaccine contains mercury in the form of the preservative thimerosal, but both contain aluminum hydroxide, which acts as an adjuvant—an agent that helps stimulate the needed immune reaction.

There is some concern that aluminum can cause long-term problems. The metal can collect in the brain, and is associated with Alzheimer's disease. It is also linked to defective mineralization and osteomalacia [softening of the bones]. Aluminum is generally well tolerated in the small quantity that is in the vaccine, but its long-term effects as a vaccine additive have not been well established. The FDA approved Gardasil in what the agency calls its "priority review process," which takes six months or less, and is used for medications with the "potential to provide significant health benefits." The available published research on Gardasil, however, was primarily from sources that were not objective. The two studies that were published and available for review were funded entirely by the manufacturer. The other studies are not available for review, but were presumably conducted by the manufacturer in its own laboratories.

Cervarix has complications of its own. In addition to aluminum, it contains a new type of additive: cells obtained from an insect cell line. When a vaccine is manufactured, the virus must be replicated in an environment friendly to it. Commonly, the cells used for this purpose are derived from yeasts, but occasionally, if a suitable yeast species cannot be found, the cells are obtained from animal species. The manufacturers of Cervarix solved some viral problems by using insect cells for replication. In the past, some viruses and other infectious agents have contaminated vaccines that have been made with animal cells. Cervarix is currently [in mid-2007] undergoing further testing for the FDA.

Concerns About Safety

When Gardasil was approved in June 2006, the FDA also recommended that it be administered to females between the ages of 9 and 26. This is despite the fact that, in the studies published to date, the vaccines were administered only to girls 15 and older. While Merck states that a smaller study was performed using Gardasil with girls between 10 and 15 years to check the immune response in that age group, the study did not assess safety beyond 14 days after administration. This study was not published, and therefore is unavailable to be read by the public and is not subject to peer review by the medical community.

The recent track record of the FDA does not instill much faith in the institution's integrity in assessing the safety of new products. The most obvious example is the recent Vioxx debacle. After having been on the market for five years, Vioxx—a prescription medication used for arthritis and acute pain (and also made by Merck)—was withdrawn in September 2004 because it was found to cause a significant increased risk of heart attack and stroke. In fact, this risk was so great that the study was discontinued before it could be completed. There is now considerable question about how much information Merck and/or the FDA concealed during the approval process for Vioxx in 1999.

Another more relevant but less well-known example of the FDA's fallibility is what happened when adolescents began taking the antidepressant Prozac. Prozac and other drugs in its class were widely prescribed to adolescents for a variety of issues, from mood disorders to bulimia. Rising concern about Prozac's side effects among young people led to numerous studies, the most recent of which was published in *Archives of General Psychiatry* in 2006. The results confirmed what had long been suspected and what other studies had shown: that Prozac caused a modest increase in the number of suicides when compared to a group of adolescents taking a placebo. Depressed teens who took Prozac were actually more likely to attempt suicide than depressed teens who took no medication at all. However, the FDA continues to recommend Prozac for pediatric and adolescent patients. Aside from calling the FDA's safety assurances into serious question, this also illustrates how a drug's proven success in studies undertaken with adults cannot be presumed to hold true for children and teens.

Gardasil and Public Health

The FDA categorized Gardasil as a drug that has the potential to provide "significant health benefits." But exactly how big is the current risk of cervical cancer in the US? There is no doubt that, every year, the disease kills American women. However, cervical cancer is not usually a quickly progressing, invasive cancer. And it generally responds well to treatment. It is also true that the vast majority of women with cervical cancer are infected with HPV. On the other hand, the vast majority of women infected with HPV never get cervical cancer.

This brings into question cause and effect. In the journal *Vaccine*, Anna-Barbara Moscicki states that, "Given the ubiquity of HPV, the most critical step in cervical carcinogenesis [cancer initiation] is not acquisition of the infection, but rather the step involving progression to clinically important lesions." In other words, it's not getting HPV that matters, it's what happens afterward. Cervical cancers diagnosed in their early stages are rarely fatal. Most fatalities are due to lack of detection and treatment.

The important keys to the prevention of cervical cancer are getting regular testing with annual Pap screens and modifying other risk factors. Getting early treatment is also important.

Regular Gynecological Exams Prevent Fatal Cervical Cancer

Regular Pap tests have reduced the rate of death from cervical cancer by at least 75 percent since the 1960s. Compared to screening for other types of cancer, Pap screening is considered by health-care practitioners to offer one of the best ratios of screening to actual prevention. It was no small feat for the public health community to establish annual Pap screening for women in the US, but it was worth the effort. Vaccination against HPV could change all of that.

The way Gardasil is being hailed in the media and advertisements, it is easy to understand how a young woman vaccinated with it might think that she has been protected against cervical cancer. Merck's campaign slogan, "One Less," implies that each woman who receives a Gardasil vaccination will be one less victim of cervical cancer. However, this idea of sure protection against cervical cancer is not only untrue but dangerous. Gardasil prevents infection by only four of the more than 100 strains of the HPV virus. This is why it is thought that the vaccines will prevent, at most, only 70 percent of cervical cancers. But what if women infected with the other 30 percent of the cancer-causing strains of HPV decide to forgo their annual exams because they have been vaccinated with Gardasil and thus believe they are protected? Overall, we would see a decrease in the number of HPV infections, but a large increase in fatalities from cervical cancer. The public research has not yet been done to see if this effect would occur.

Greg Zimet, PhD, a clinical researcher at the Indiana University School of Medicine, has published several articles in medical journals about Gardasil. Although in favor of the vaccine, he concedes that a reduction in the number of women getting annual Pap tests might be an "unanticipated cost" of the vaccine's approval by the FDA; he emphasizes that "this does not change the need for regular Pap testing." After 30 years of success in the public health sector with Pap tests and cervical cancer screenings, it would be a shame to backslide now.

Compare the statistics of cervical cancer in the US to those in places where the rates of cervical cancer and death from it are still high. In Haiti, the poorest country in the Western Hemisphere, cervical cancer accounts for nearly half of cancer deaths; in the US, 2.5 percent. Regular screenings make the difference. In places such as Haiti, where most people cannot afford and/or have no access to regular screening, Gardasil may be just what the doctor ordered. However, Gardasil is an expensive vaccine, and is not marketed toward or currently available to these poorer populations; and in the US, it may actually cause more deaths from cervical cancer.

Another issue that only long-term research will resolve is how long a single vaccination with Gardasil will provide protection. So far, trials have shown that it sustains an immune response for five years, but it is still far too early to know whether immunity granted by Gardasil is lifelong or temporary. Knowing this will have a large impact on when, how, and if young women should be vaccinated.

A Costly Experiment

Do Gardasil's potential benefits outweigh the risks? Perhaps, but only time will tell. If it is similar to the hepatitis B vaccine introduced some years ago, it is still far too soon to know. "As shown by research on hepatitis B vaccination, many key answers only became known at least ten years after the vaccine first became available," states Eduardo Franco, of McGill University, Montreal, Canada, in *Vaccine*.

The bottom line is that we don't yet have enough information to know whether young women should be vaccinated en masse with Gardasil.

We know that it is effective in conferring immunity against HPV. What we don't know is if it is safe to use with adolescents. Nor do we know anything about its long-term safety and efficacy with any age group. Nor do we know if mass vaccinations will cause a decline or an increase in deaths from cervical cancer. Considering how little we know, are we ready to make an entire nation of preadolescent girls the subjects of a vast experiment? At $360 for the full series of three injections, it will be challenging to even find the funding for a national vaccination campaign. Gardasil is one of the highest-priced vaccines ever marketed. It is a costly risk to take.

CHAPTER 2

Teens and Sexual Orientation

Teens Are Discarding Labels

Ritch C. Savin-Williams

Ritch C. Savin-Williams is a practicing psychologist and profes-sor of developmental psychology at Cornell University, specializ-ing in adolescent sexual identity development. He has served as an expert witness in court cases involving gay adoption, same-sex marriage, sodomy laws, and the exclusion of gays from the Boy Scouts of America. His most recent book, The New Gay Teenager—*from which this excerpt is drawn—examines new trends in teen sexuality and critiques the psychological model used to research gay adolescence, which tends to view homosexu-ality as a risk factor rather than a valid developmental trajec-tory. Savin-Williams tracks changes in how adolescents have conceptualized their sexual identities over the past 30 years, not-ing a marked shift away from rigid categorization of both their own orientations and those of others. This shift has proven equally threatening to both the gay and straight political estab-lishments. Savin-Williams concludes that, in many circles, the politics of identity have either dropped by the wayside or become so actively detrimental to young adults living the lives they choose, that they have chosen to discard traditionally empower-ing labels altogether.*

Despite the speculations of some clinicians, the idea that it is healthy for an adolescent to identify with a sexuality has not been proved. Clinicians are fond of assuming that not adopting a label is unhealthy, that it may be an indication of possible psychological problems. An individual's reluctance to embrace a sexual identity, they say, suggests that the person is in denial, afraid to confront his or her sexual reality. Yet how do we square this view with the overwhelming evidence—

produced by these same clinicians—of alarmingly high levels of depression, substance abuse, dangerous sexual activities, and suicidality among those young people who self-identify as gay? Is it possible that self-identifying gay youth are more unhealthy than nonidentified same-sex-attracted young adults?

I believe this is entirely possible. Some gay teens come out "loud and proud" as an act of self-affirmation, and some nonidentified same-sex-attracted young people are in hiding for self-destructive reasons. But it is also true that some declare their sexuality as a cry for help from horrific circumstances and that others are psychologically healthy because they have bases for self-definition other than sexuality that are more developmentally appropriate.

Is it possible that our advice to same-sex-attracted young people has been wrong, and that perhaps we should be encouraging them *not* to identify as gay? Right-wing politicians and ministers advocate this position—but they want more. They want adolescents to *give up* their same-sex sexuality. In this they are naive, because giving up one's sexuality is impossible to do.

As millions of teens are demonstrating, it's possible not to identify oneself sexually and still embrace one's sexuality. The inclination to shun "being gay" can be an adaptive strategy for emotional survival during hostile times and in dangerous environments. Or not identifying can be indicative of a self-loving and wise adolescent. Or perhaps the motivation to self-identify or not has little to do with one's mental health. Gay identity can be indicative of both good and bad mental health. . . .

Any idea that adolescent same-sex sexuality is all the same, or that it has predetermined developmental trajectories and consequences, is belied by the life narratives of contemporary teenagers. Their sexuality is but one facet of an interactive system that makes up their lives. Any presumption that teens have identical developmental pathways because they share a same-sex sexuality or that their sexuality is equally important to various teens' sense of self is not only implausible, it is a gross misrepresentation of their lives. The notion of there being a single gay identity or lifestyle is, in short, absurd, especially to adolescents.

To overcome our prevailing misperceptions, we must demystify sexuality and see it as a valid developmental topic, not a clinical risk factor. Sexual development should be seen as a legitimate, growth-promoting, and core aspect of what it means to be an adolescent. At the same time, we must understand that the extent to which sexuality defines identity spans from all-important (it is what I am) to a mere biological fact.

Refusing a Label

A recent survey of a Massachusetts high school revealed that over 11 percent of the students ascribed to themselves at least one aspect of homoeroticism. Seldom, however, did they report having sex with someone of the same gender or identifying as gay. Fewer than 3 percent were willing to assume a gay or bisexual label. In a California high school, 6 percent reported that they "know that I am homosexual or bisexual" and an additional 13 percent said that they frequently or sometimes wonder if they are homosexual.

Naming sexuality as a means to stamp a personal and positive understanding [on]to a life narrative is a relatively recent development. Identifying as gay first became prevalent among those who came of age in the 1970s and 1980s. As Gil Herdt and Andy Boxer put it, people who gave themselves such an identification signified "living with their desires, not in hiding and alienation, but out in the public, in the light of social day—leading to adaptation and greater creative fulfillment than they could have imagined at the beginning of the process."

Although some young people today might also get these advantages from identifying as gay, perhaps especially if they live in secluded, conservative regions of the country, many others object to self-labeling. Some find their sexuality to be more fluid than that permitted by constructed models of sexual identity. Some have notions of what a gay person looks like, acts like, and believes—and it's not them. They cannot or do not want to attribute these features to themselves. Some are philosophically opposed to the idea of placing their sexuality into "identity boxes." To them, the mere creation of sexual categories reifies the labels across time and place and exaggerates differences that don't exist. Some young people give themselves an uncommon or unrecognized label (e.g., two-spirit) or one that encompasses multiple identities (e.g., bi-lesbian). Many simply find the labels an annoyance. One young woman told me:

> I felt there just was no need for labels, so I didn't tell anyone. But when I was in tenth [grade] I got interested in this other girl and we were in a romantic relationship. Then I began to define myself differently, more definitely, that it was more real. I just thought labeling was silly, but then people began to ask me for a label. To calm them I said bisexual.

> I had wanted to be friends with this girl and then I became more and more interested and then a crush developed. This did not change my self-concept ... What I wanted to say was that I simply was just in a relationship with a woman. People asked because most of my friends were involved in the gay community and most of my friends were lesbian or gay.

In her work with young people, Beatrice Green observes adolescents who engage in same-sex behavior and yet "refuse the politics of sexual identity, arguing that these are the issues of the older generation. They claim the right to love and have sex with whomever and in any way they want." She refers to them as the "new Act Up generation" and speculates that although they might threaten both the gay and the straight establishment, "they may be the future in a post-identity politics society." I agree.

These young people are repudiating the appropriateness and artificiality of dichotomous definitions of sexual identity as they challenge cultural definitions of gay lives. Gay and straight categories may have been fine for their parents, but not for them. Youth culture is permeated by nuance, especially with regard to sexuality. Sexual behavior and sexual orientation flow within various gender expressions and changing definitions of what is gay, bisexual, and straight. If pushed, they might agree to vague terms such as "queer" or "not straight." Their preference is to not call themselves, or their futures, anything at all. They refuse to label themselves because they wish to separate sexual desire from the friction of politics. One person who was interviewed for a popular article on the "polymorphous normal" asserted that sexuality is not about politics but about pleasure and happiness. Another eschewed identity categories because "my experience is continuous. It's not compartmentalized into poetry and sexuality and rational thought. We confuse the map with the territory."

Some of these young people have been called "queer," defined by anthropologist Melinda Kanner as individuals intent on "destabilizing conventional categories, subverting the identities derived from and normalized by heteropatriarchy. Queerness defies binary and fixed categories such as homo-/ heterosexual, female/male, even lesbian/gay. Queerness, in both social performance and in lived identities, interrupts both convention and expectations." Most teens, however, do not think of themselves as queer or appreciate the word. They simply reject the potentially life-altering repercussions of such a label.

Their rejection of label designations is motivated by many things—for philosophical reasons, because the labels seem irrelevant and uncharacteristic, in an attempt to avoid homophobia, or because the label is simply felt to be inaccurate. Some may believe that their current attraction or relationship is a "special" one, an aberration that implies little about them or their sexuality. Others fear the consequences of being gay and so remain unlabeled and closeted, perhaps coming out later in their lives. We know little about these nonidentified teens, but we know they exist.

In a 2001 interview, actor and filmmaker Jason Gould was asked about being gay, coming out, and disclosing his sexuality to his famous parents, Barbra Streisand and Elliott Gould. Jason, who recalled having his first "gay impulse" at age eight, says that he has not come out as gay because he has never said to himself, "Oh, I'm gay." He denies living a closeted life or being ashamed of who he is. "I'm pretty comfortable with my sexuality," he says, adding,

> You know, the more I understand my own sexuality the more I . . . I mean I don't mind being called gay, because I'm certainly attracted to men. But I also think that it's limiting. I think that within the gay community—and as a member of the gay community—it's limiting for us to stereotype ourselves. Attraction is more complex than the terms gay, straight, and bisexual. And I hope that eventually people will evolve into accepting a broader understanding of attraction.

Gould's refusal to declare a sexual identity is apparently not a function of internalized homophobia or self-hatred or fear. He has declared his sexuality—he is attracted to men; he simply finds the term "gay" an inadequate descriptor of his sexuality.

Jason Gould is not alone. Comedian Rosie O'Donnell doesn't appreciate the adjective "gay" permanently attached to her name. Being attracted to other women, she says, was never a "big deal for me." Sophia of MTV's *Road Rules* downplays her sexuality: "It's not a big deal to me because I don't make it a big deal . . . It's just part of who I am."

The balkanization of sexuality, according to one writer, is especially prevalent among artists, students, cultural explorers, and young women. They prefer an alternative, self-generated identity label or no label at all rather than those typically offered in research investigations. Two of these groups, young women and cultural explorers, in particular have not been well served by standard sexual taxonomies.

Young Women and Fluidity

Inflexible, distinct boundaries rarely apply to young women's sexuality. A young woman's most enjoyable sexual fantasies might be of other women while her most enjoyable sex is with men—or vice versa. Young women are more likely than young men to incorporate partners of both sexes in their behavior and fantasies. When shown explicit sex films, lesbians and heterosexual women do not differ in their subjective and genital arousal to either male-female or female-female sex scenes, and the highest arousal for both groups of women is to heterosexual sex scenes. In their research, Meredith Chivers and her colleagues suggest that women, regardless of sexual orientation, have a "nonspecific" pattern of sexual arousal. That is, although heterosexual college women might say that they prefer heterosexual over female-female and male-male erotica, their actual genital arousal to sex scenes indicates no significant preference of male-female over female-female scenes. They prefer and become more aroused by female-female than male-male sex scenes. By contrast, gay and heterosexual men show a strong preferred-sex ("categorical") pattern. Gay men are more aroused by male-male than male-female scenes, and heterosexual men are more aroused by male-female scenes, although heterosexual men react most strongly to female-female erotica. Perhaps as a result, women are less apt to be stigmatized for engaging in same-sex behavior.

In eighth grade Stephanie and Lolita were best friends. Stephanie recalled that

Lolita would sleep over a lot and one night she was talking
about her boyfriend Juan and talking about sex. I was pretending to know more than I did. We had been very affec-
tionate, like most girlfriends. I asked her how he kissed her,
and so she kissed me like her Juan did. This was quite a
shocker. From then on we kissed a lot when we got together,
and began touching and caressing. To make it "okay," one of
us would be the boy. Was penetration with our fingers but
never oral sex. She's straight as far as I know.

Never talked about it. I can't tell what Lolita is, but I was
the only girl she did anything with. We never said we were
lesbians. I kind of knew that it was not right, but it felt
okay. Mom caught us in bed and this was a big uproar. We
had gotten together every day after school for six to seven
months but Mom made that more difficult.

Stephanie's attitude was that her experience with her friend
was just a kid experience. Lots of peers were having sex, only
with guys, so having sex was not unusual.

Once a young woman recognizes that she's not totally
straight, there is little guarantee that she'll declare herself to
be lesbian or bisexual. In an attempt to identify "authentic"
lesbians, researchers have traditionally relied on what they believe has worked for identifying gay young men: the achieve-
ment of developmental milestones. But . . . such models won't
distinguish lesbians who maintain their lesbian identity over
time from those who don't. It is more informative to examine
patterns of attraction and behavior.

Over the course of eight years, nearly two thirds of the
young women Lisa Diamond interviewed changed identity labels at least once, often because "sexual identity categories
failed to represent the vast diversity of sexual and romantic
feelings they were capable of experiencing for female and
male partners under different circumstances." Some of these
women expressed their ambivalence by viewing their sexuality
as fluid. Love depends on the person, they told her, not the
gender of the person.

Those women Diamond studied who relinquished their lesbian or bisexual identity for a heterosexual or an unlabeled status had similar developmental histories. What differed was their *interpretation* of their sexual experiences. The women who would not be labeled described their sexuality as fluid and expressed uncertainty about their future sex lives. Those who changed to a heterosexual label had lower levels of same-sex attractions and behavior throughout the study than did the other women. A heterosexual identification was, for them, a viable solution to the "problem" of their nonexclusive attractions and behavior.

Relinquishing a sexual identity label, however, did not mean that these women relinquished their same-sex sexuality. Their same-sex attractions and behavior were real, not a phase. All maintained that they might identify as lesbian or bisexual in the future. Diamond noted that

> [t]hese findings are consistent with the notion that identity relinquishment does not represent a fundamental change in sexual orientation itself, but rather a change in how women interpret and act upon their sexual orientation ... Nonexclusivity and plasticity in women's attractions and behaviors potentiate multiple transitions in identification and behavior over the life course.

In short, attempts to fit an adolescent girl's "complex, highly contextualized experiences of same-sex and other-sex sexuality into cookie-cutter molds of 'gay,' 'straight,' and (only recently) 'bisexual'" are doomed to failure. The exception of these young women to follow sexual identity models of identity progression simply reflects the complexity of their lives.

Cultural Explorers and Alien Notions

A similar disconnect between orthodoxy and life histories is evident for young people in non-U.S. cultures and subcultures within the United States. In reviewing the cross-cultural evidence, Fernando Luiz Cardoso and Dennis Werner conclude,

"People vary tremendously in their same-sex behaviors, in their sexual desires, and in the ways they define themselves. Cultures also differ widely in the ways they define and treat these relationships and the people who engage in them." Western definitions of sexuality are viewed as exceedingly rigid. For example, as one writer notes, in some communities "same-sex relationships are defined between individuals and may involve sexuality, eroticism, and very intensive friendships and emotions. Men can therefore hold hands in public or sleep naked in the same bed together." One Iranian remarks that in his culture labels for sexuality are relatively rare.

It is not difficult to find cross-cultural examples of a homoerotic life that are not identified as such. One has been referred to as "Mediterranean homosexuality." In a culture with this type of sexuality, according to Iñaki Tofiño, a gay activist in Catalonia, there is a "large zone of liberty for homoerotic activity between males, but no such thing as a 'homosexual identity' as such." The sexes are often separated during adolescence and young adulthood; homoerotic friendships, alliances, and physical contact are not uncommon. A person's identity (for both men and women) is not usually defined by what one does sexually or who one falls in love with. To do so would be to deny the more legitimate cultural prescriptions for identification based on religion, region, or ethnicity. To "come out as gay" makes little sense in such a culture. To attach a gay persona "in every situation is an alien notion" and can often be problematic when sex is not part of the public discourse.

Tofiño argues that Western notions of a public or private gay identity that one carries from one situation to the next are not necessary for large-scale cultural changes to take place. For example, in Spain few identify as gay; yet sexual orientation is a category that enjoys broad protections in that country's Penal Code, which acknowledges same-sex couples and provides gays with protection against hate crimes.

An example within the United States of how a gay identity has been subverted is described in a recent *New York Times Magazine* article. Author Benoit Denizet-Lewis explores the world of African American young adult men who have sex and romantic relationships with men and who are forging an "exuberant new identity" based not on their sexuality but their skin color and culture.

> Rejecting a gay culture they perceive as white and effeminate, many black men have settled on a new identity, with its own vocabulary and customs and its own name: Down Low ... [T]he creation of an organized, underground subculture largely made up of black men who otherwise live straight lives is a phenomenon of the last decade ... Most DL men identify themselves not as gay or bisexual but first and foremost as black. To them, as to many blacks, that equates to being inherently masculine.

A DL identity signifies a virulent rejection of a gay identity associated with "drag queens or sissies." One eighteen-year-old whom Denizet-Lewis spoke with clearly wants this separation. "Gays are the faggots who dress, talk and act like girls," he said. "That's not me." These men acknowledge the sexuality in their lives, but being DL is not perceived as merely another sexual identity label. It is about "being who you are, but keeping your business to yourself." It is a selection of ethnic affinity over sexuality and masculinity over femininity.

The majority of young people of both sexes with same-sex desire resist and refuse to identify as gay. We know little about them because they usually opt out of research, educational programs, and support groups. Their desire is not to stand out ... but to be as boring as the next person, to buy an SUV and to fade into the fabric of American life.

Most School Libraries Do Not Support Gay Teens

Debra Lau Whelan

As the proportion of teens identifying as lesbian, gay, bisexual, or transgender (LGBT) has increased, Gay-Straight Alliances have spread to most schools, and school administrators have become increasingly sensitive to LGBT issues. Nonetheless, relatively few school libraries offer gay-themed literature, nonfiction books about gender and sexuality, or access to LGBT-related online resources. Such resources are valuable to any health curriculum, as well as being important to the healthy development of LGBT students, and foster tolerance among the student body as a whole. This article from the School Library Journal *highlights the special challenges facing school librarians, who must balance often conservative community standards with the reality of their students' needs, and in the process examine their own fears and biases in the materials they choose to stock and highlight.*

Erica Barton has liked girls since kindergarten, but it took her eight years to tell the world that she was gay—and coming out in a small town like Lawrence, KS, wasn't easy.

There was the time in fifth grade when the emotional pain was so great that Barton slit her wrists and ended up in the hospital for months. Then there were the years of anxiety over the reaction of her family, friends, and peers. Getting jumped by a bunch of school kids was another fear that weighed heavily on her mind. "It put me through hell," says Barton, now a 17-year-old senior at Lawrence High School. "It was harder than I thought it would be."

Despite all she went through, Barton doesn't regret coming out at 13. "I decided to stop hiding myself and to go for it," she says. "Times have changed, and it's a lot easier now because people are more accepting."

Thanks to the growing number of gay characters on TV shows like *Desperate Housewives, Will and Grace*, and MTV's *Real World*—and the more than 3,000 Gay-Straight Alliances in high schools nationwide—Barton is one of the three million gay, lesbian, and bisexual youth who are coming out as early as middle school rather than in college or later in life. With as many as 20 percent of all adolescents having some degree of same-sex orientation, according to Ritch Savin-Williams, author of *The New Gay Teenager*, it's surprising that many teens still say they don't have access to lesbian, gay, bisexual, and transgendered (LGBT)—related resources in their schools.

Few Schools Offer Gay-Related Resources

According to the 2003 National School Climate Survey, a biannual study by the Gay, Lesbian, and Straight Education Network (GLSEN), an organization which ensures safe schools for LGBT students, only 50 percent of students say they have access to community LGBT Web sites, such as *Parents, Families, and Friends of Lesbians and Gays*, and gay-related resources in their media centers.

The numbers are hugely disappointing because so many gay kids find school libraries to be safe havens and still go there to find resources even though information is so widely available elsewhere, says Dan Woog, founder of OutSpoken, a Connecticut-based support group for LGBT teens and author of *School's Out: The Impact of Gay and Lesbian Issues on America's Schools.*

Even Alex Yip, who came out two years ago [2004] in a big city like San Francisco, says he's forced to take the bus to the main library to find gay-themed titles because his high school library and local branch just don't offer enough. "I always knew I was gay and that I wasn't like other people," says the 17-year-old senior at George Washington High School. "There were so many times when I felt so invisible, trapped, and insecure because I wasn't living up to my family's expectations. [Books] made me feel better about myself."

Gay Youth Find Solace and Identity in Books

Barton, who says she's probably read every gay-themed book in her school library, agrees. "Reading gets me in touch and makes me feel better knowing that there are other people out there like me," says the teenager, adding that books such as *Night Diving* by Michelene Esposito and *Love Rules* by Marilyn Reynolds made her feel "very comfortable coming out."

Arla Jones, Barton's librarian at Lawrence High School and founder of the school's Gay-Straight Alliance, has become the school's de facto counselor for gay teens because of her extensive gay literature collection and the fact that she's a lesbian herself. Her school library's Web site says "of the 85 to 90 percent of teens who aren't themselves gay or lesbian, almost every one of them has a friend, teacher, parent, future coworker, or significant associate who is." Kids are way ahead of adults, Jones says. "They are more sophisticated about having gay friends and of gay people who are out. Most students couldn't care less; it's the adults who are really uptight." Her advice? Don't make a big deal out of building a gay collection—just make sure books are well cataloged so kids can easily find them.

Former American Library Association (ALA) President Ann Symons, who until recently was a media specialist at Juneau Douglas High School in Alaska, knew she had failed as a librarian when she read the introduction to *Young, Gay, and Proud!* Written by one of her former students, Don Romesburg, Symons discovered that he couldn't find anything on his school library shelves as he struggled to define his sexuality while growing up. Symons, who learned her lesson, advises taking a "proactive stance" to starting an LGBT collection by "building the collection you feel you need and dealing [with the controversy] later."

Fear and Bias Prevent Librarians from Building LGBT-Themed Collections

Internet-filtering software on school computers and the lack of federal and state funding for school libraries are partly to blame for the inadequate school library services for gay teens. But librarians themselves are the most likely culprits because they dislike controversy. "There's nothing more important to the school administration than keeping its name out of the news," says Pat Scales, director of library services for the Governor's School for the Arts in Greenville, SC, and a frequent speaker on intellectual freedom. Gay teens may stress the importance of identifying with characters in books, but when someone like Laurie Taylor, the Fayetteville, AR, parent who recently challenged 58 sexually explicit books in her local school library, gets national attention, the spines of many librarians and administrators suddenly go limp.

What's the risk? Michael Glatze, the editor-in-chief of *YgA*, a bimonthly magazine with a circulation of 10,000 that targets young gay America, says it best: "Librarians shouldn't be in the business of denying information." Without vital books and resources, gay kids can end up in high-risk situations involving online predators or turn to drugs to help them cope. "Confidence comes from information and knowing that you're not alone," Glatze says. Just 13 years ago, when Glatze was a high school student in Tumwater, WA, he was so starved for information about anyone like himself that when a *Time* magazine cover article about homosexuals hit the newsstands, he kept a photograph of a gay couple featured in the article under his pillow for a whole year.

Unfortunately, some media specialists have personal objections to gay literature and are quick to throw the concept of intellectual freedom out the window, and others are oblivious to it because they're former teachers without graduate degrees in information science, says Jones. For those media specialists who claim they don't have enough money or insist they're restricted to buying books that support the curriculum, those are just excuses, says Symons. All librarians have resources to purchase recreational materials and you could easily argue that gay-themed books fall into the health curriculum. "Kids are looking for books about themselves," Symons adds. "If you are buying a limited selection of everything, purchase at least one or two books that are well written and well reviewed for gay teens."

Gay Literature Fosters Understanding

The consequences of failing to build a gay literature collection can be enormous, says Riley Snorton, GLSEN's spokeswoman. For one, it could discourage the teasing and bullying that still goes on in so many schools. An alarming 82 percent of the estimated 887 13- to 20-year-olds recently surveyed by GLSEN say they've been verbally harassed at school because of their sexual orientation, and more than 90 percent say they frequently hear remarks such as "faggot," "dyke," or "that's so gay."

Although physical attacks are less common, Kat Forrest, a 16-year-old junior from Olathe, KS, is one of the nearly 20 percent of teens who say they were assaulted because of their sexual preference. Hostile school environments have an adverse effect on LGBT teens' ability to learn, damaging their sense of belonging, their academic performance, and their educational aspirations, says Kevin Jennings, GLSEN's executive director. Students who report frequent harassment, for example, have grade point averages that are more than 10 percent lower than those who did not, and those who are verbally attacked are less likely than other students to say they plan to attend college, the survey says.

Matthew Shepard, the 21-year-old University of Wyoming student who, in 1998, was robbed, beaten, tied to a fence and left to die, all because he was gay, has put a public face on the horrible crimes that are committed by ignorant people, says Glatze. "The mistake we often make about young adult literature is that it's only for the student who can identify with it," adds Scales. "But straight kids need to read *Annie on My Mind* [Farrar, 1982, by Nancy Garden] and *Deliver Us from Erie* [HarperCollins, 1994, by M. E. Kerr] to learn about tolerance."

Gay Literature in School Libraries Is Often Challenged

In the three decades in which Scales has defended the right to read, she's found a direct correlation between a political shift to the right, which started in the 1980s during the Reagan Administration, and a huge spike in the number of censorship cases. Overall, there's been a tenfold increase in the number of book challenges across the country, and since most are objections to sexual content, homosexual-themed books are often targeted, Scales says. The situation has gotten so bad, that one-third of the top-10 book challenges last year were gay titles.

Librarians such as Jeff Blair at Olathe High School admit to a certain level of self-censorship. In 1993, the Olathe School District was at the center of a lawsuit involving the censoring of *Annie on My Mind*, the novel that began a trend of high-quality young adult literature with homosexual protagonists who were not punished for their sexuality. While the district lost the case because of its "obvious bias against homosexuality," says Blair, the school board ended up instituting a selection policy for all district school libraries, essentially bringing in a censor to approve the purchase of all books. "Literally thousands of books go through her," says Blair, referring to the four high schools, eight middle schools, and 32 elementary schools that must still get a green light from the "library coordinator." "She can reject any book, and she doesn't have to have a reason."

Fortunately, few districts have such a policy. Most of the 547 recorded book challenges filed with ALA in 2004 didn't succeed, which means that librarians often prevailed in most censorship cases—if they managed to show some fortitude. "We need to fight them like you would fight a bully," Scales says. "But it takes a lot of courage, and very few people want to go through the bother."

Librarians may want to take comfort in the knowledge that the law is on their side, says Glatze. Administrators who question the purchase of gay literature may think twice if they hear about Jamie Nabozny, a gay student who won a $900,000 out-of-court settlement in 1996 when he sued his Ashland, WI, school district for violating his rights by not protecting him from years of harassment by fellow students. Nabozny was kicked, mock-raped, and suffered continual verbal abuse. As a result, many administrators who fear lawsuits understand the need to create safe environments for gay students, says Woog, a varsity soccer coach at Staples High School in Westport, CT, who helped found the state's first high school Gay-Straight Alliance. Celebrating Gay Pride Week, Gay History Month, GLSEN's Day of Silence, an annual vow of silence to bring attention to harassment in schools, and ensuring your school has policies in place to protect students' sexual orientation and gender identity are a few ways to build awareness.

A Wide Selection of Quality Gay-Themed Books Exists

The growing number of gay-themed titles for young adults over the last five years means kids today shouldn't have to scrounge for information. Fortunately for librarians, quality books are everywhere. "What safer place is there to get this information than in a book?" asks Lynn Evarts, a media specialist at Sauk Prairie High School in rural Wisconsin whose library boasts an extensive fiction and nonfiction gay-themed collection. Besides, says Evarts, it's easy to defend books with literary merit.

"A gay book has to be good in order to get published," says author David Levithan, who wrote *Boy Meets Boy*, adding that books by writers Julie Anne Peters, Alex Sanchez, and Francesca Lia Block attract both gay and straight readers, win prestigious awards, and receive favorable reviews. Major children's book publishers such as Random House, Scholastic, and Penguin Putnam realize that gay literature has become so mainstream that their plots no longer hinge around a teen coming out—they're just high school students who happen to be gay. "There are gay teens in every high school, whether they're in or out, or struggling with their sexuality," says Levithan. And that's why it's so critical to "normalize" everything, says author Savin-Williams. "We're talking about millions of kids who have same-sex attractions to varying degrees," he adds. "So the point is to demystify same-sex sexuality and to understand that it is a normal part of human life."

Sexual Orientation Is Part of Self-Discovery

Heather Corinna

Heather Corinna has written extensively about erotica, the Internet, and human sexuality. She is the founder of the Scarleteen *Web site, the Internet's premier source of sex-positive education for teens and young adults, and author of the book* S.E.X. *In the following advice column, Corinna makes clear that, above all, it is important not to let sexual orientation be an overriding, limiting factor in one's life. One's sexual orientation develops over time, she argues, and does not dictate one's life course or personality. According to Corinna, regardless of how traumatic it might seem to reveal a non-heterosexual identity to one's friends and family, the constant discomfort of living a concealed life—or one of denial—is ultimately far more destructive.*

H apless, London asks:

I'm 17 yrs old, not sexually active, never had a boyfriend (and I'm more than fine with it). Ever since my friend came out as bisexual, I've had this horrible feeling that I might be too. I've thought sexually about women for a few years now, and occasionally look at female porn. I just assumed this was normal, straight-girl activity, even though I don't think about guys as, um, graphically. Since my friend came out I've found myself attracted to certain women, not just sexually but romantically, as well as guys.

I just DON'T WANT to be lesbian or bi. I have no problems with them, but I don't want it to be part of my life. I'm terrified I'll have to acknowledge it—my family's loving but straight-laced and wouldn't accept it, for one thing, and it's just not the

Heather Corinna, "I Think I Might Be Bisexual, But I Really Do Not Want to Be," *Scarleteen*, August 29, 2007. Reproduced by permission.

way I planned my life to run. I don't know how to explain it without sounding bigoted, but I don't want to deviate from the social "norm". I don't know what to do. Is there any way of— checking, some how? Is the Kinsey Scale accurate? Am I just imagining it since my friend came out?

Please tell me what to think, because I don't know what to do. Thanks in advance. I'm so glad for this website.

Heather replies:

For most people, whether we're talking about sexual orientation or something else, trying to live a life as anything but yourself is more painful than living a life working to come to peace with something about yourself that you or others are uncomfortable with.

Really, if you read the stories of older bisexuals and homosexuals who tried to live their whole lives in the closet, they'll break your heart seven ways to Sunday. I've heard a ton of them, on the page and firsthand, and even after over two decades of being exposed to them, I still can hardly bear most of them.

Let's assume for a moment that you *are* bisexual, even though that may or may not be the case.

Sexual Orientation Is Not Limiting

You still get to choose who you partner with. You still get to opt into heteronormativity if that turns out to be what you really want. You still get to decide how little or how much your bisexuality—and your sexuality period—plays a part in your life and your identity. You still get to choose who you share information about your sexuality, your attractions and your sexual relationship with. You still get to have whatever sort of life you've planned (with the understanding that on so many levels, the plans we have for our lives in our youth often differ from how our lives play out realistically).

Most importantly, you still get to be exactly who you are, no matter who that is, or to whom that person is attracted.

Understand that you're hardly alone in these feelings: there are a pretty rare few of us who are gay, lesbian or bisexual who haven't strongly wished we weren't at one point or another, mostly—and often *only*—just because the world we live in can still be so discriminatory and unfriendly towards us, and being anything but heterosexual—in a similar way to being anything but white—can sometimes be something that makes our lives more difficult than it might be otherwise. But ultimately, as most folks will tell you who felt that way and tried to be something they weren't instead, trying to be a person you aren't makes things far more painful and difficult.

Sexuality Reveals Itself Over Time

Regardless, whether you are bisexual, lesbian or not, this isn't something you need to get panicked about or really worried about right now. Sexual orientation—even for straight folks—is something that tends to reveal itself over time, and no one is required to be any level of out while they figure it out. There's no reason to figure out how it fits into the plans of your life, or to put off those plans, right now: after all, the plans you make for your life should be more about you than your relationships, especially if you're not actually in one. Relationships should fit the whole of your life, not the other way round.

Certainly, plenty of women who are and/or identify as heterosexual and who look at pornography look at a myriad of types of it: while our fantasies sometimes have something to do with our realities, they just as often do not. But to be frank, if you've had a few years of thinking about women both sexually and romantically, and those feelings are stronger and more persistent than they are for men, it's not very likely that you're solidly heterosexual. Mind, more people are bisexual—whether they choose to partner same-sex or not—than those who are heterosexual and homosexual, even though more people identify as heterosexual and choose to live their lives only dating opposite-sex. And since you've had those feelings for a couple of years, it seems unlikely your friend coming out somehow made you suggestible to this.

But you have plenty of time to figure all of this out: as much as you want or need. What I'd suggest is that you give yourself that time, and in the meantime, no matter *what* you turn out to be, you perhaps spend some time looking at why you have the biases you've got, and who they're really about. In other words, your family having any level of homophobia isn't about you—save that theirs likely rubbed off on you, too—it's about them. Any sort of avenue for your life that might only seem to have room for you as a member of a heterosexual couple is about cultural biases: not about you. Because those things are unjust and discriminatory doesn't mean there's anything wrong with being lesbian or bisexual: rather, it means there's something wrong with the way some aspects of culture and some people view sexuality and orientation and romance. And while things certainly still aren't just ducky for non-heteros, even just over the last thirty years, things have improved pretty drastically. For all we know, in ten or twenty more, we may see the same velocity of improvement.

Living in Denial

No matter what, it's really a lot more scary and limiting to think about a life where you'd try and live in denial of an aspect of yourself on purpose, or try and be someone you're not, especially with something you really have no control over. I mean, often I sure don't want to be short, nor am I that thrilled to see the effects of gravity on my backside, and sure, once or twice in my life I've wished my sexual orientation was different than it was, but as Popeye always said, *I yam what I yam*, and that's about all there is to it. It'd be a pretty big waste of my energy and time to try to pretend things about me that just are are not, and doing that would make me a lot less happy than just accepting even the things I don't like or wish were different.

So, for now, why not just invest your energy on getting to know who you are and accepting yourself? As you go through that process you can figure out how to manage and deal with what you discover, but there's little sense in putting the horse before the cart or freaking out about what you could be and how people will react until you just relax and find out for yourself what you really want and who you are.

Experimenting with Sexuality Can Be Confusing

Megan

Sex, etc. is an award-winning magazine and Web site published by Rutgers University and written for, and primarily by, teens. It is the most recent offshoot of the university's twenty-five-year Network for Family Life Education program. Sex, etc. is best known for publishing first-person accounts written by teens about the realities of their own sexual choices. In this article, seventeen-year-old Megan talks about her early physical attractions and experiments. Although she knew she was attracted to girls, she felt obliged to conceal this, even as she continued to explore her homosexuality. Ultimately, she found that even when she had grown to accept her sexual orientation, the straight-bias of sex education programs left her entirely unprepared to handle her own same-sex romantic relationships.

It was my 11th birthday and I had a bunch of girlfriends coming over. In my head I thought up possible scenarios about how the night may go. I knew that one thing would definitely be thought about, what guys we thought were cute. There was only one problem, I didn't like any of the guys, in fact I thought that a lot of the girls who were coming over were more attractive than the guys I knew. We were in 6th grade and I knew nothing about being gay, but what I *did* know was that none of the other girls were "into" girls. And so I quickly thought up the first guy I knew and forced myself into pretending I liked him.

That's when my charade began. For years I would pick a guy and become obsessed with him. I would make a point

Megan, "I'm Taboo: Am I the Only One Who Wants to Talk About How Hard It Is to Be Single, Gay, and Young?" sexetc.org, September 4, 2007. Reproduced by permission.

that everyone knew how much I "liked" said guy. But in the back of my mind I always worried, what if this guy ended up liking me? I didn't want to date a guy! And in truth under it all I would look at my girlfriends and pine over them. Would I ever tell them? No!

Experimentation and Shame

In 8th grade there came a HUGE turning point in my life. A good friend of mine was moving to Texas, and so I decided to throw her a going away party. I invited a majority of her friends, including a few girls I didn't know well at all. One girl who showed up, we'll call her Sam, was a little "out there." I didn't really like her much but then she started talking about how she had kissed a girl. I was shocked that she was okay with just saying that so blatantly! And the best part was, no one freaked out! In fact, all the other girls seemed really interested in hearing about her. Maybe I wasn't the only one who didn't think she liked guys . . . Maybe I wasn't wrong.

Later that night we ended up in my room with blankets drawn over the windows and in front of my door and the radio blasting so my parents couldn't hear us playing truth or dare. The fact that I had never been kissed was revealed and I could feel the tension in the room as my best friend, we'll name her Jessica, was dared to kiss me. Well, Jessica never turned down a dare sooo . . . she leaned over and gave me a peck. Well, that just led to more and more specific dares until I had gotten my first "real" kiss and then quite a few more. Pretty soon we weren't playing truth or dare anymore, we had moved onto more and more kissing games.

I think that all of us had wondered before that night what it would be like to kiss another girl. And for once in my life I didn't feel like such a creep. Unfortunately all the girls were kind of ashamed of what we had done because we were in 8th grade and being gay, or bi, or lesbian just was not talked about. And we all thought it was wrong and so we were sworn to secrecy. But I had a few parties after that, and they all led to the same thing. By then I knew I liked girls, but since everyone else was so ashamed I decided that it must be wrong. So I continued my game of liking random guys and the parties soon stopped. I was terrified that I might really be gay and I knew that it must be wrong. So I never revealed my secret. Well . . . that is until this past year in 11th grade.

Unprepared for Same-Sex Relationships

I knew a few girls who were openly gay and two girls I liked were dating each other. By now, I was okay with the fact that I was gay. Alright, not "okay" but I was in a better place than I had been. I came out to my family, spare my dad, and wasn't exactly embraced. But they have become more accepting and I am now comfortable with who I am and where I am in my life. I'm gay and that's okay. Now I have a new problem, they didn't teach being gay in sex-ed. It was never mentioned, and never brought up. So I feel like a little kid with no clue about sex or dating or any of that. I have liked one girl for almost 5 months now, but I have no clue how to go about telling her. I know that she's gay, but I don't know how same sex relationships work. I am hopeless in that area, and I think a lot of that has to do with the fact that gay relationships were never discussed with me. I'm gay, I'm clueless, and I'm taboo.

CHAPTER 3

The Risks of Teen
Sexual Behavior

Pregnant Teens Are More Likely to Engage in Risky Behavior

Jacqueline Collier and Holly Blake

Jacqueline Collier and Dr. Holly Blake are researchers at the Centre for Population Sciences at the University of Nottingham, England. Their interests include patient education, child and maternal health services, and children's quality of life. Based on research from both the United States and the United Kingdom, the following report gives insight into how another industrialized first-world nation is coping with the consequences of unprotected teen sex. Collier and Blake have found that a significant portion of pregnant adolescents engage in unprotected intercourse and other sexual behavior that increases their risk of contracting sexually transmitted diseases during and after pregnancy. Additionally, Collier and Blake describe an increase in the incidence of repeat teenage pregnancies, which suggests that pregnant teenagers are a high-risk group that warrants special attention from healthcare workers. Fortunately, because pregnant teens are already in contact with healthcare providers, additional services can immediately be extended to them.

Sexual health is an important public health issue with increasing attention being paid to the development of national policy strategies for teenage pregnancy and reproductive health. Current research suggests geographical variations in teenage conception and births with higher rates in areas of greater social and economic deprivation. Teenage motherhood has been identified as having a negative effect not only on

Jacqueline Collier and Holly Blake, "Sexual and Reproductive Health in Pregnant Teenagers Presenting for an Antenatal Care or for Termination," *Current Paediatrics*, vol. 16, June 2006, pp. 211–215. Copyright © 2006 Elsevier B.V. All rights reserved. Reprinted with permission from Elsevier, conveyed through Copyright Clearance Center, Inc.

health but also on education, labour market attachment and pay. Even after accounting for any educational differential, the economic effects may be substantial suggesting teenage mothers have difficulties combining labour market participation and child rearing. This may in turn contribute to cycles of deprivation. Teenage pregnancy is a problem of social exclusion and therefore central to government policy on tackling health inequalities. It is a complex social issue associated with low academic attainment and poor career prospects, poor physical and mental health, low self-esteem, social isolation and poverty.

The UK Teenage Pregnancy Strategy aimed to reduce by 50% the 1998 under 18 conception rate (47.1/1000) and establish a downward trend in conception rates for under 16s by 2010. However, data on the Teenage Pregnancy Unit website suggest these targets are proving hard to meet with the under 18 rate falling only slightly to 42.3/1000 by 2003, and the under 16 conception rate reducing from 9/1000 to 8/1000.

Pregnant teenagers are sexually active and are more accessible for health interventions than any other sexually active group as they are identified and known through their contacts with family doctors, abortion service providers and/or to midwives and obstetricians. Those who deliver a live birth continue to be in regular contact with health visitors. Thus, this high-risk group is identifiable, and there are opportunities to provide a targeted intervention aimed at improving their sexual health. In addition, improving outcomes and reducing repeat pregnancies during the teenage years has been identified as a valid target in the Social Exclusion Unit's report on teenage pregnancy.

Pregnancy has been described as a 'window of opportunity for sexual risk reduction' yet scant research can be identified about sexual risk-taking among pregnant/mothering teenagers. A recent review of the literature states that 'there exists remarkably few interventions aimed at reducing sexual risk among pregnant/mothering teens . . . and no intervention targeting both STD/HIV and repeat pregnancy has been published.'

Teenage Pregnancy and Sexually Transmitted Infections (STIs)

Many of the adolescent population seen by paediatricians may be sexually active. In 2000, a research article showed that over a quarter (26%) of 16- to 19-year old females reported being under 16 years of age at first sexual intercourse. Young adults are those most likely to report STIs, for example in the Health Protection Agency's report 'Mapping the Issues, HIV and other STIs in the United Kingdom: 2005', 36% of all female chlamydia diagnoses in 2004 were in the 16–19-year old age group and 37% to those aged 20–24 years. Interestingly this document did not report on data for those under 16 years of age. However, for the year 2000, it is possible to identify official government statistics identifying 1,035 new cases of chlamydia and 228 new cases of gonorrhoea in the under 16s.

With regard to the other marker of sexual health, teenage pregnancy, there were approximately 8,000 conceptions to girls under the age of 16 years, 34,200 conceptions to 16- and 17-year olds and 56,400 to 18- and 19-year olds reported in England and Wales in 2003. Of those under the age of 16 years, 57% resulted in an abortion, the remainder continuing with the pregnancy.

Whilst risk of STIs and risk of pregnancy are not the same, STIs and unintended pregnancy both require sexual contact, usually unprotected intercourse or failed use of contraception. From the data available, teenage pregnancy appears to be a greater likelihood than sexually transmitted disease for the younger teenagers.

However, it should be highlighted that, contrary to some viewpoints, pregnancy is not a time of reduced sexual risks and rates of STI are high among pregnant teenagers. The UK pilot study of opportunistic screening for chlamydia found that [approximately equal to] 10% of teenagers undergoing antenatal care and [approximately equal to] 14% of those attending for termination of pregnancy tested positive. Generally, sexually active women have been found to have a very poor knowledge of chlamydia, despite it being the most common STI and one study showed that teenagers attending an abortion clinic had significantly poorer knowledge of chlamydia than women attending family planning clinics. Teenagers presenting at genitourinary medicine (GUM) clinics have been found to be at high risk of unplanned pregnancy. A study following those presenting at a GUM clinic (who stated that they were not pregnant and were not wanting to become pregnant) identified that 28% of these teenagers became pregnant within a year.

The majority of pregnant teenagers appear to remain sexually active. Niccolai et al. found that two-thirds of pregnant teenagers reported vaginal intercourse in the last 30 days, which was less than non-pregnant teenagers (66% compared with 77%). However, of the sexually active teenagers in this study, 88% of the pregnant teenagers were having unprotected intercourse compared with 62% of those who were not pregnant. In this study pregnant and non-pregnant teenagers did not differ in terms of other sexual risk behaviours except the lack of condom use. Furthermore, 20% of the pregnant teenagers had chlamydia or gonorrhoea diagnosed during their pregnancy. Niccolai et al. also cited a further study that found that the proportion of pregnant teenagers who were sexually active did not differ from the proportion of non-pregnant adolescent mothers who were sexually active. Again risk behaviours were higher, with only 12% of pregnant teenagers reporting use of a condom the last time they had sex compared with 43% of non-pregnant adolescent mothers.

The relationship between pregnancy and STI is demonstrated. Teenagers with STI are at risk for pregnancy as well as pregnant teenagers being at risk of STIs. After the pregnancy the risks seem to remain. Postpartum teenagers have been identified as a group vulnerable to STIs. Pregnant teenagers recruited during their last trimester were followed-up 6 and 12 months and new chlamydia and gonorrhoea infections were 14.3% at the 12-month follow-up (9 months postpartum). This prevalence was higher than the comparison group of non-pregnant sexually active teenagers, although not significantly higher. The results of this study strongly suggest that the postpartum teenagers are particularly vulnerable to new STI infections during that first year postpartum.

Teenage Pregnancies and Subsequent Repeat Pregnancies

Many pregnant teenagers continue to be sexually active whether they continue with the initial pregnancy or not and rates for repeat teenage pregnancies are high. One UK study found that teenage mothers may be eight times more likely to conceive a further pregnancy than other teenagers. Another UK study of teenage pregnancies in general practices found that 20% had been pregnant at least once before, earlier UK research involving 101 teenagers aged 17 years or less showed that at least 13% had been pregnant before. For those who continue with the pregnancies it has been found that it is not first teenage birth that leads to poorer outcomes, rather it is the consequences of a second teenage delivery that may be detrimental to health. When comparing the birth outcomes of 110,223 non-smoking mothers aged 15–19 and aged 20–29, among first births the only significant difference in adverse outcomes by age group was for emergency caesarean section, which was less likely among younger mothers. However, second births in women aged 15–19 were associated with an increased risk of moderate and extreme prematurity and also still birth.

Many pregnancies subsequent to teenage pregnancy lead to termination. Although not all teenage pregnancies are unwanted the high numbers terminating later pregnancies indicate that many are unplanned. In 2001, in England and Wales, 12% of legal abortions to teenagers followed an earlier teenage birth and 12% followed a previous legal abortion as a teenager. These two groups are not mutually exclusive and cannot tell us how many of the teenagers presenting for termination have been pregnant before. However, one might suggest that only a minority have had both a previous birth and a previous abortion as teenagers, and one might postulate that about a fifth of all teenage abortions are to teenagers who have conceived previously. This is a worryingly high number of repeat pregnancies, probably unplanned, and resulting in termination. This has increased over the preceding 11 years, both in terms of absolute numbers and with regard to the proportion, as in 1991, 8% of legal abortions to teenagers followed an earlier birth and 8% followed a previous legal abortion.

Preventive Interventions

The evidence clearly demonstrates that pregnant teenagers are at high risk of both STIs and unintended conceptions. Interventions over the last decades have not reduced the levels dramatically. Despite the high interest in the area we do not clearly understand the reasons for the continuing high teenage pregnancy rates and increasing numbers of STIs.

Partly this may be because one of the highest risk groups, the already pregnant teenagers, are currently not targeted sufficiently in government policy development; for example, when the Counterpoint report explored young people's perceptions of contraception and seeking contraception advice and provided considerable insight, no pregnant (or previously pregnant) teenagers seem to have been interviewed.

Abstinence can be advised for prevention of STIs and repeat pregnancy. However, abstinence-only programmes are primarily found in the United States and may not be transferable to the UK. Moreover, reviews of the evidence as to their efficacy report mixed findings with one concluding that abstinence programmes may have a positive effect on attitudes among adolescents, but are not proven to have a significant effect on sexual behaviour. Further to this, the evidence regarding efficacy is commonly reported with regard to delay in sexual initiation, and the limited evidence of the effect of an abstinence programme on existing sexual activity suggests that positive outcomes were especially limited among the sexually active, a finding identified as emphasising the difficulties of reaching adolescents who are already at high risk for pregnancy.

There is a need for individualised sexual health advice to be provided for sexually active teenagers who have already conceived, and healthcare professionals need to consider the costs and benefits of differing methods of contraception. Hormonal contraceptive methods are most effective at preventing pregnancy but ineffective in preventing transmission of STIs. Male condoms are most effective at preventing STIs but are only effective in preventing pregnancy in ideal conditions with consistent use. However, in conditions typical of the sexual activity of many teenagers (i.e., inconsistent use) these methods are not effective at preventing pregnancy.

Key to the sexual health of sexually active teenagers then appears to be the value of dual protection. That is, the use of hormonal methods to reduce the risk of pregnancy, and the use of barrier methods to reduce the risk of STIs. Recognition of the dual roles that contraception can play (prevention of conception and prevention of infection with STIs) has prompted both the World Health Organisation and the International Planned Parenthood Federation to advise that sexual and reproductive health programmes integrate information and education on protection against STI/HIV with that on protection against unwanted pregnancy. However, this does not appear to be reflected in the current practise of those providing sexual healthcare for pregnant teenagers, whether the teenagers are presenting through antenatal services, or for termination of the pregnancy. Evidence suggests instead that current routine practice regarding the health promotion activities associated with the prevention of future pregnancy and STIs appears to be unsatisfactory in relation to pregnant teenagers. The repeat pregnancies and high rates of STIs provide ample evidence of poor use of the contraceptive pill, low condom use, risky sexual behaviour and poor knowledge levels.

One report identified that midwives did not commonly report antenatal discussion of sexual health issues as 'sexual health' was equated with contraception, with the result that pregnant teenage girls often may not be given the advice to avoid unprotected sex until they enter the postnatal period. The findings of Niccolai et al. suggest that this is clearly too late. A further study revealed that teenage girls presenting for termination of pregnancy, though a clearly identified high-risk group for chlamydia, continue to lack sufficient sexual health advice, as only 25% were given a full discussion on contraception and information about STIs. Furthermore, younger teenagers may be reluctant to approach sexual health services, and appear to be selective in where they choose to obtain sexual healthcare. One study examined those under 16 years attending various clinic settings in Manchester and showed that whilst 6% of the community GUM clinic clients were 15 years old or younger and 1% of clients attending the hospital-based GUM clinic were of that age group, the majority attended a specialist young persons clinic, with 12% of clients attending regular Brook clinics being less than 16 years.

The NHS Evidence Briefing 'Teenage pregnancy and parenthood: a review of reviews' identified evidence from the United States of the effectiveness of involvement, outreach and support for parents and families. However, this is not currently reflected in the UK literature and further work is needed here. A study in the United States showed that a home-visitation programme by nurses, aimed at improving: the outcomes of pregnancy; the physical and emotional care of their children; clarification of goals and problem solving to promote work, education, and family planning, was associated with a reduction in subsequent pregnancies/births and with a delay in subsequent pregnancies. The majority of participants in this study were aged 16–24 years. Studies in the United States have shown the success of home visiting in reducing numbers of repeat teenage pregnancies, but such intensive programmes may not be sustainable in mainstream service delivery.

Pregnant teenagers are sexually active and are more accessible for health interventions than many other sexually active groups, as they are identified and known through their contacts with family doctors, abortion service providers and/or to midwives and obstetricians. Those who deliver a live birth continue to be in regular contact with health visitors. Thus this high-risk group is identifiable and there are opportunities to provide a targeted intervention aimed at improving their sexual health. In addition, improving outcomes and reducing repeat pregnancies during the teenage years has been identified as a valid target in the Social Exclusion Unit's report on teenage pregnancy.

Implications

Given this evidence of unwanted second and subsequent pregnancies and the association between STIs and teenage pregnancy, it is imperative that the sexual health of already pregnant teenagers is not neglected further. Meade and Ickovics' recent systematic review of sexual risk among pregnant and mothering teens in the United States identified some clear conclusions, primarily: that behaviours that lead to teen pregnancy also place young women at risk for STIs and repeat pregnancy; compared with the broad literature on adolescent sexual risk behaviour our understanding of sexual risk in pregnant/mothering teens lags far behind; that teen pregnancy is a marker for future sexual risk behaviour and adverse outcomes; that pregnant/mothering teens need dual protection interventions; and that pregnancy may provide a critical 'window of opportunity' for sexual risk reduction. As we have identified that pregnant teenagers are a potentially high-risk group, yet can be more accessible for health interventions than many other sexually active groups, this is a group of clients whose sexual health should be considered a priority by all healthcare professionals that they encounter.

In summary, research in this area indicates that a substantial proportion of pregnant adolescents engage in unprotected intercourse and risky sexual behaviours that may increase their risk for acquiring STIs during pregnancy and beyond. Although some research findings cannot be generalised as they focus on clinic-based convenience samples or minority adolescents residing in urban areas, there is sufficient evidence that repeat teenage pregnancies are on the increase, and that STIs are also common in this client group, teenagers that have already conceived. These adolescents therefore represent an important sector of the population in which to target interventions.

Practice Points

- Pregnant teenagers often continue to be sexually active, and often do not use barrier methods (to prevent STIs)

- The provision of sexual health advice for pregnant teenagers is often poor

- Pregnant teenagers are continuing to be unsuccessful in following safe sex advice both during and after the pregnancy

- The risk of STI such as gonorrhoea and chlamydia is high

- Rates for repeat teenage pregnancy are high

- Many pregnancies subsequent to early motherhood lead to termination

- This group is more accessible to health intervention as they are already in contact with service providers

Research Directions

- A scoping exercise to identify current provision of sexual health advice to pregnant teenagers

- Evidence from the UK of the effectiveness of involvement, outreach and support for parents and faculties

- Evaluations of individualised programmes of sexual health advice

- Work on the cost-effectiveness of interventions

Teen Oral Sex Is Increasing

Tim Harford

Tim Harford is an English economist, journalist, and author of two books on economics: The Undercover Economist *and* The Market for Aid. *In his work, Harford uses the tools of economic theory to examine problems not generally thought to be economic in nature. In this article, Harford analyzes the increase in oral sex among teens in terms of* incentives *affecting consumer choices. (In economics, an incentive is any specific factor that influences a rational consumer's decisions, preferences, or actions.) Harford argues that, as children are increasingly bombarded with messages emphasizing the dangers of sexually transmitted infections [STIs] and pregnancy, the incentive for teens to choose oral sex—which offers a decreased risk of STIs and no risk of pregnancy—naturally increases.*

"Parents, brace yourselves." With those words, Oprah Winfrey introduced news of a teenage oral-sex craze in the United States. In the *Atlantic Monthly,* Caitlin Flanagan wrote, "The moms in my set are convinced—they're certain; they know for a fact—that all over the city, in the very best schools, in the nicest families, in the leafiest neighborhoods, 12- and 13-year-old girls are performing oral sex on as many boys as they can."

Are they right? National statistics on teen fellatio have only recently been collected, but the trend seems to be real. Johns Hopkins University Professor Jonathan Zenilman, an expert in sexually transmitted infections . . . reports that both the adults and the teenagers who come to his clinic are engaging in much more oral sex than in 1990. For men and boys as recipients it's up from about half to 75 to 80 percent; for women and girls, it's risen from about 25 percent to 75 to 80 percent.

In some quarters, that might be regarded as progress, but how you feel about it probably depends on whether you are a teenager or a parent of teenagers. I am more than a decade away from being either and so regard myself as a neutral in this debate. Moreover, as an economist, I feel uniquely qualified to opine on why it is happening.

Incentives Affecting Sexual Decision-Making

Now, there is no shortage of explanations: Perhaps everyone just thought that if it was good enough for Bill Clinton and Monica Lewinsky, it was good enough for them. But an economic explanation would instead start with the premise that this is a response to changing incentives. What sort of incentives have changed?

Schoolchildren are now bombarded with information about the risks of sex, particularly HIV/AIDS. Oral sex can be safer than penetrative sex: It dramatically reduces the risk of contracting HIV and reduces the effects of some other sexually transmitted infections (although you can still pick up herpes, warts, and thrush). An infection that might have made a girl infertile instead gives her a sore throat.

The rest is basic economics. When the price of Coca-Cola rises, rational cola-lovers drink more Pepsi. When the price of penetrative sex rises, rational teenagers seek substitutes. Perhaps we shouldn't be surprised that even as the oral-sex epidemic rages, the Centers for Disease Control and Prevention reports that the percentage of teenage virgins has risen by more than 15 percent since the beginning of the 1990s. Those who are still having sex have switched to using birth-control methods that will also protect them from sexually transmitted infections. Use of the contraceptive pill is down by nearly a fifth, but use of condoms is up by more than a third. The oral-sex epidemic is a rational response to a rise in the price of the alternative.

The Rational Teenage Sex Drive

Now, this is a glib explanation. A real economist would want a tighter hypothesis and serious data to back it up. That economist might well be Thomas Stratmann, who, with law professor Jonathan Klick, has pushed the idea of the rational teenage sex drive. Their hypothesis is that if teenagers really did think about the consequences of their actions, they would have less risky sex if the cost of risky sex went up. They discovered a very specific source of that higher risk: "In some states, there are abortion-notification or -consent laws, which mean that teenagers can't get an abortion without at least one parent being informed or giving consent." If teenagers are rational, such laws would discourage risky sex among teens, relative to adults.

Klick and Stratmann claim to have found evidence of exactly this. Wherever and whenever abortion-notification laws have been passed, gonorrhea rates in teenage and adult populations start to diverge. When it becomes more troublesome to get an abortion, teenagers seem to cut back on unprotected sex.

Economic nerds may be interested to know that the Klick-Stratmann statistical technique owes much to the one used by [famed economist] Steven Levitt and John Donohue to show a link between legalized abortion in the 1970s and lower crime in the 1990s.

The rest of us may be wondering what to make of it all. On the one hand, good news: Teenagers are finding safer ways to get their kicks. On the other, it suggests that teenagers believe one of the most serious consequences of an unwanted pregnancy is that their parents will find out. If teenagers are avoiding unsafe sex, it may not be for the best reasons.

Oral Sex Among Teens Is Not Increasing

Cathy Young

Cathy Young is a contributing editor and columnist for the liber-tarian magazine Reason, *and author of the book* Ceasefire: Why Women and Men Must Join Forces to Achieve True Equality. *She writes on many facets of politics and culture, often focusing on feminist and gender issues. In this article, Young explores a purported "epidemic" of fellatio among teen girls, and the ac-companying outcry from all quarters, including both vocal femi-nists and staunch conservatives, condemning the U.S. culture's victimization of teen girls. Young argues that these stories of "rainbow parties" are highly unlikely and that they tend to run counter to established studies. These studies include* Child Trends *analyses from 1995 and 2002, which found no significant change in the reports of oral sex among teens, and a broad 2005 study by the National Center for Health Statistics and the Centers for Disease Control and Prevention, which revealed that boys and girls gave and received oral sex in equal numbers. Young con-cludes that these stories gain traction—despite being difficult to verify and directly contradicted by well-documented studies— because they both prey on parental fears and feed adults' fasci-nation with the sex lives of teens.*

The teenage oral sex panic began in the late 1990's. It is in some ways a part of the Clinton legacy—more specifically, the Clinton-Lewinsky legacy. It was Clinton's most famous line ("I did not have sexual relations with that woman, Miss Lewinsky") and the subsequent debate on whether receiving oral sex qualified as "sexual relations" that produced the ap-

Cathy Young, "The Great Fellatio Scare: Is Oral Sex Really the Latest Teen Craze?" *Reason*, vol. 38, May 2006, pp. 18–20. Copyright © 2006 by Reason Foundation, 3415 S. Sepulveda Blvd., Suite 400, Los Angeles, CA 90034, www.reason.com. Reproduced by permission.

parently shocking disclosure that a lot of teenagers were not only engaging in oral sex but regarding it as not quite sex.

Worse: According to press accounts, America's young Monicas weren't just having oral sex; they were having it in circumstances that would raise Hugh Hefner's eyebrows. In July 1998, the *Washington Post* ran a front-page story with the headline, "Parents Are Alarmed by an Unsettling New Fad in Middle Schools: Oral Sex."

An Epidemic of Casual Fellatio

Its main example was a scandal in an Arlington, Virginia, school, where a group of eighth-graders would get together for parties at which boys and girls paired off for sexual activities that eventually progressed from petting to oral sex. There were also a couple reported instances of public fellatio, on a school bus and in a hallway, that reached school authorities "through the student grapevine."

From here, it was only a short step to tales of "rainbow parties" where several girls wearing different colors of lipstick would take turns servicing a boy until their lipstick traces formed a "rainbow" of rings. In 2003, this peril was explored by Oprah herself, with the help of *O* magazine feature writer Michelle Burford, who interviewed 50 girls, some as young as 9, and painted a frightening picture of kiddie debauchery. "Are rainbow parties pretty common?" inquired a rapt Oprah, to which Burford replied, "I think so. At least among the 50 girls that I talked to . . . this was pervasive."

Burford did not say whether the girls had told her they themselves had attended such parties, or if they had simply heard rumors. Nor was any proof produced of what was actually said in those interviews.

All these stories invariably depicted the oral sex as almost entirely one-sided, with girls giving and boys receiving. "One more opportunity for male satisfaction and female degradation in the name of adolescent sexual curiosity," harrumphed

Baltimore Sun columnist Susan Reimer. In this familiar script, feminists saw girls as victims of male dominance, while conservatives blamed feminists and Clinton, whose bad example supposedly sent kids the message that fellatio was OK.

The Epidemic Is a Myth

Now the "rainbow party" tale—which has never been substantiated and may well have originated with that *Washington Post* story—has become the subject of a novel, Paul Ruditis' *The Rainbow Party*, published last summer [2005] by Simon Pulse, a young adult division of Simon & Schuster. While conservatives have widely denounced the book as yet another excrescence of our licentious culture, its message actually seems to be one of almost old-fashioned moralism: The girl who plans the party is humiliated when hardly anyone shows up, then punished with a gonorrhea infection to boot.

Ruditis' novel has prompted a new round of hand wringing. On the Fox News Channel's *Hannity & Colmes*, radio psychologist Judy Kuriansky asserted that teenagers had been telling her about rainbow parties for years on her show, and assured the shocked hosts that yes, those parties really were going on. "Unbelievable," sputtered Sean Hannity.

Unbelievable, indeed. For one, as Caitlin Flanagan points out in a lengthy review essay in the *Atlantic*, the different colors of lipstick would almost inevitably smear and destroy the supposedly sought-after rainbow effect. Besides, a boy would have to be a sexual super-athlete to complete the circuit. The "current oral-sex hysteria," Flanagan writes, "requires believing that a boy could be serviced at the school-bus train party—receiving oral sex from ten or fifteen girls, one after another—and then zip his fly and head off to homeroom, first stopping in the stairwell for a quickie to tide him over until math."

Succumbing to the Hysteria

Unfortunately, while Flanagan—who has recently drawn attention with her tart, often thoughtful critiques of feminism—

starts on a skeptical note, she turns around about a third of the way into her sprawling, nearly 9,000-word tract and succumbs to the hysteria. She dismisses the tales of orgies and rampant anonymous blow jobs as nonsense, noting that she has been able to find only one verified account of a girl performing oral sex on multiple boys at a party. Yet she thinks the reality is bad enough.

"We've made a world for our girls in which the pornography industry has become increasingly mainstream," Flanagan writes, "in which Planned Parenthood's response to the oral-sex craze has been to set up a help line, in which the forces of feminism have worked relentlessly to erode the patriarchy—which, despite its manifold evils, held that providing for the sexual safety of young girls was among its primary reasons for existence. And here are America's girls: experienced beyond their years, lacking any clear message from the adult community about the importance of protecting their modesty, adrift in one of the most explicitly sexualized cultures in the history of the world. Here are America's girls: on their knees."

What is the basis for this Wendy Shalit-style outburst? A study by the National Center for Health Statistics and the Centers for Disease Control and Prevention, released in September 2005 found 25 percent of 15-year-old girls and half of 17-year-olds had engaged in oral sex. While the survey did not include children under 15, the report noted that in a survey several months earlier, only 4 percent of adolescents 13 to 14 years old said they'd had oral sex. (Did any of this represent an increase from the past? Probably not: A Child Trends analysis of data from surveys of unmarried males ages 15 to 19 in 1995 and 2002 found no significant changes in reported rates of oral sex experience.)

While Flanagan talks about sex "outside of romantic relationships," the September 2005 study said nothing about the context [relationships] in which these activities took place—casual encounters or steady dating.

Girls and Boys Are Equal Partners

The study did say something about one aspect of the alleged oral sex craze, something that contradicts conventional wisdom. Girls and boys, it turns out, are about equally likely to give and to receive. Actually, at least among younger adolescents, boys overall reported more oral sex experience than girls, but both boys and girls were more likely to report receiving oral sex than giving it—which suggests a lot of respondents are fibbing.

This finding was so counterintuitive that some "experts" chose to disbelieve it: Joe McIllhaney Jr., chairman of the Medical Institute for Sexual Health, told the *Washington Post* he doubted that girls were really enjoying oral sex: "I'd like to know a whole lot more about the pressure boys put on girls." Others, such as James Wagoner of the reproductive health organization Advocates for Youth, argued that the new data subverted the stereotype of boys as predators and girls as prey.

How does Flanagan deal with this information? By refusing to deal with it. Throughout the article, she assumes girls are only the givers, referring to "this strange new preference for unreciprocated oral sex" and even speculating that girls, ill-served by our modesty-unfriendly culture, have taken to giving oral sex in order to keep their own sexuality protected from male encroachments. (Boys, Flanagan adds, aren't vulnerable to the emotional repercussions of sex the way girls are, so as a mother of boys she has little personal concern about the oral peril.)

Are some kids having sex too soon, and with too many partners, for their own emotional and physical well-being? Almost certainly. But the majority do not inhabit the sexual jungle of worried adults' imaginations. The teenage fellatio craze exists mainly among adults. To those in the audience who are not worried parents, it provides both sexual and moralistic thrills; it plays both to the prurient fascination with teenage girls gone wild and to the paternalistic stereotype of girls as victims. It does very little to help either adolescents or their parents deal with the real problems of growing up.

Sexual Education Should Address Emotional Consequences

Ilene Lelchuk

Ilene Lelchuk has written for the San Francisco Chronicle *since 2000, primarily covering the intricacies of city government and local social issues. Throughout 2006 and 2007, she focused on youth and family trends, such as developments in foster care and innovative approaches in San Francisco's public schools to address children's issues, including obesity and gender confusion. In this article, Lelchuk reports on the findings from an early 2007 study conducted by researchers from the University of California, San Francisco. The study explored teens' mixed emotional responses to having oral and vaginal sexual intercourse. Although a majority of the students reported enjoying sex, they also indicated that, while oral sex carried fewer perceived risks, it was also less pleasurable and emotionally fulfilling, with more than one-third feeling bad about themselves afterward. Likewise, while slightly fewer students felt bad about themselves after vaginal intercourse, a larger proportion felt guilty or used. The authors of the study suggest that emotional health is not given nearly enough consideration in the design of sexual education programs.*

We know teens are having sex and opting for oral sex over intercourse because they think it's safer. Now a team of UCSF [University of California, San Francisco] researchers may be the first to analyze how it makes adolescents feel.

Ninth- and 10th-graders surveyed at two California high schools between 2002 and 2004 revealed mixed emotions that for many included guilt and feeling manipulated.

Girls were more likely than boys to feel bad about themselves afterward and to "feel used." Boys were more likely than girls to say sexual activity made them feel self-confident and popular.

"We tend to focus on the health consequences of having sex, like pregnancy and STDs, but we also need to talk to them about all the emotional consequences," said UCSF pediatrics Professor Bonnie Halpern-Felsher, senior author of the report published this month in the journal *Pediatrics.*

Teens Often Feel Guilty After Sex

Of the 618 students her team followed from their freshman year, 44 percent reported having intercourse or oral sex by the end of 10th grade. The report focuses on the surveys from those 275 students and the differing effects of intercourse and oral sex, which researchers said has become more common because teens believe it carries fewer physical and emotional risks.

A majority said they enjoyed sex. The teens who engaged only in oral sex reported fewer problems with sexually transmitted diseases, pregnancy, guilt and their parents—but less resulting pleasure, self-confidence or intimacy with their partners.

Forty-one percent said they felt bad about themselves later, nearly 20 percent felt guilty, and 25 percent felt used. By comparison, 36 percent of those who had intercourse reported feeling bad afterward, 42 percent felt guilty and 38 percent said they felt used.

But boys and girls were affected differently. Girls were twice as likely as boys to report feeling bad about themselves, and nearly three times as likely to feel used, according to the UCSF research. Boys were more than twice as likely as girls to report experiencing popularity and self-confidence. (Because the gender differentiation arose in a statistical analysis called a regression, it isn't possible to contrast gender responses with absolute percentages.)

Casual Sex Can Be Stressful

"This report suggests what many teens come to find out on their own: Even if sexual activity seems casual, it often is not," said Bill Albert, deputy director of the nonprofit National Campaign to Prevent Teen Pregnancy in Washington. "A casual hookup on a Friday night might not feel that way a month down the road."

The teens were surveyed, with parental permission, every six months during 9th and 10th grades. Researchers did not disclose what schools the students attended or where in California they lived.

By some counts, teenage oral sex is now more prevalent than intercourse, although teen sexual activity overall is declining and more teens are delaying sexual activity, compared with a decade ago.

More than half of 15- to 19-year-olds surveyed in 2002 had had oral sex, according to the National Survey of Family Growth. And the National Youth Risk Behavior Study has shown a decline in the proportion of high school students having intercourse. Forty-seven percent surveyed in 2005 said they had ever had sex, down from 54 percent in the 1991 survey.

Sex therapist Darcy Luadzers, author of two new advice books for teens about how to navigate the sexual world, said she sees the emotional toll firsthand in her practice. The adults she treats have problems that often date back to regretful teenage experiences, she said. Also, in collecting adolescents' stories for her books *Virgin Sex for Girls* and *Virgin Sex for Guys*, she found most of them were regretful about their first experiences.

"We just don't talk about the emotional consequences enough," Luadzers said.

Luadzers, who has raised five teenagers and lives in South Carolina, said the downsides of teen sex hit home when one of her sons was in middle school and reported that several girls in his class offered him oral sex if he'd become their boyfriend.

Teachers and Parents Neglect Emotions

According to a 2002 federal survey, teens started having intercourse at age 17 on average. One in 7 girls started by age 15, down from 1 in 5 in 1995, according to the National Survey of Family Growth.

Teens hanging out at the Metreon video arcade and the Westfield San Francisco Centre food court one afternoon this week seemed to bear out the research results when asked whether they wanted to be interviewed about sex: The girls were shy and the boys full of bravado. Two boys, ages 14 and 17, who spoke on condition of anonymity, said they became sexually active when they were 12.

They said it seems like sex is prevalent and casual among students at their schools, San Francisco's Washington and Phillip Burton high schools. And in sexual education classes, they said, teachers talk mostly about biology, rarely about emotions. The girls hanging out didn't want to talk at all about sex.

The UCSF researchers concluded that parents and educators should talk more with their children about all consequences—physical, social and emotional—of oral sex as well as intercourse. The authors suggest it might be easier to convince adolescents to delay sex if adults acknowledge the benefits, such as feelings of intimacy, and then suggest other ways to achieve them.

"It gives them tools to make better decisions," Halpern-Felsher said.

Teenage Sexual Activity

Of 618 California high school students tracked by a UCSF pediatric research team between 2002 and 2004, 44 percent reported having intercourse or oral sex by the end of 10th grade.

The finding was in line with national studies showing that almost half of teens from 15 to 17 years old have had oral sex—42 percent of girls and 44 percent of boys.

Even among the two-thirds of teens nationwide ages 15 to 17 who have not had intercourse, 21 percent of boys and 18 percent of girls have had oral sex.

Teens have mixed emotions after oral sex and intercourse: 41 percent of kids in the UCSF survey who had oral sex said they felt bad about themselves, compared with 36 percent who reported feeling bad after intercourse. On the other hand, almost 42 percent of teens who had intercourse told UCSF researchers they felt guilty, compared with 20 percent who said they felt guilty after oral sex.

CHAPTER 4

Personal Perspectives on Teens and Sex

I Have an STI

Holly Becker

Holly Becker is a teenaged contributor to Sex, etc., *the award-winning sexual-health magazine and Web site published by Rutgers University.* Sex, etc. *is well known for its first-person accounts written by teens. In this piece, Holly recounts the fragile self-esteem and misunderstandings that led to her having unprotected sex and contracting herpes. Along with a graphic description of the physical pain from a pelvic inflammation caused by her untreated infection, she also details the social and emotional turmoil she experienced when her infection became known to her peers. Finally, Holly explains how she copes with herpes physically, emotionally, and in her relationships.*

"A sexually transmitted disease will never happen to me."

I used to tell myself this—before I contracted the herpes virus. But first, let me start with a little story.

August 2000. His name was Derek [name has been changed], and I knew him from work. He was 22 and I was 17. Tall and skinny, he wasn't the cutest guy, but his character made him attractive. He was funny, very charismatic, and he treated me well. He made me feel like I was someone to be noticed. To guys at work, he would say, "Wow, boys, look at that girl. Isn't she somethin'?" He gave me special attention to boost my self-esteem. He would say other things like, "You're so beautiful." Whenever other girls were around, he'd ignore them and only pay attention to me. Derek was my friend, and I trusted him.

About a month after we started hanging out, we had sex for the first time. I asked him that question: "Have you been

Holly Becker, "Herpes: My Story," sexetc.org, April 18, 2007. Reproduced by permission.

tested?" He swore to me that he had. "I'm clean," he said. He didn't get specific about when he was last tested. I still asked him to wear a condom.

A little while into the sex, I could tell he hadn't put on a condom. I knew then that I'd made a mistake, but I didn't stop him. I was embarrassed and afraid of being rejected. I thought about treatable infections, like chlamydia, and figured that if Derek had anything, then I'd already gotten it and the damage was done.

September 2000. I started noticing some differences with my body—pains and smells that hadn't been there before. Derek and I still slept together without a condom. I kept thinking that the damage was already done. And I wasn't serious with him; we were very casual. So I didn't say anything. I figured there was no way I could get anything serious, like herpes, HIV, or syphilis. I was also nervous. I'd never been to a gynecologist, just to my doctor for checkups, and I was too afraid to tell my mother what I was doing.

November 2000. The symptoms were unbearable and the pain got worse. I couldn't urinate without screaming out loud. My abdominal pain brought tears to my eyes. While working alone one day, I got very sick. I called my mother and asked her to come get me. I finally told her about my symptoms. We went to a gynecologist first thing the next morning.

Thank God for my supportive mother. She held my hand while I screamed in pain as the doctor took a Pap smear and culture. It felt like torture. Imagine this: your entire insides are swollen and inflamed, and someone puts just a slight amount of pressure on that swelling and inflammation. It feels like someone just rammed a sword into you. I have never felt anything so horrible.

After seeing the open lesions that were down there, the doctor said that there was a good chance it was genital herpes.

He was certain that I had a raging case of Pelvic Inflammatory Disease (PID), which is sometimes caused by an STD.

"Genital herpes?" I thought. "He must be wrong; he's just trying to scare me. Am I the type of girl who gets herpes? Who is?"

How You Contract Herpes

Herpes is a sexually transmitted disease that's caused by the herpes simplex virus (HSV). HSV-type 1, or oral herpes, normally causes fever blisters on the mouth or face. HSV-type 2, or genital herpes, usually affects the vagina, penis, and/or anus. Herpes viruses are usually "inactive" and cause no symptoms. But sometimes, the viruses cause "outbreaks" of fluid-filled blisters and lesions.

Once a person is infected with herpes, he or she has it for life.

Genital herpes is not uncommon. If you look at the percentage of adolescents and adults who have it, you might even consider it normal. Across the United States, 45 million sexually active people ages 12 and older—that's one out of five of the total adolescent and adult population—are infected with HSV-2. And genital herpes is more common in sexually active females—approximately one out of four of us are infected with it.

But even though herpes is so widespread, the general feeling in society is that there's something really wrong with you if you become infected. Like you had to sleep with at least five people, instead of just the one person who gave it to you. The common perception is that you're obviously a "slut" if you get genital herpes. But I slept with one person and I got it.

Living with Herpes

Most people don't know that you can live with and manage herpes. Every once in a while, especially when you're stressed, you'll get outbreaks of tiny lesions or blisters on your genitals.

If you have sex during this time, you're likely to transmit the virus to your partner. You can also transmit herpes to a sexual partner before and after you break out in sores, until the sores have healed. But you can't get herpes from a toilet seat, a towel, or clothing. These are myths.

If you're going to have oral sex or intercourse, always use a latex condom or dental dam the correct way. But remember, condoms don't completely protect you from herpes. If a guy has genital herpes, for instance, the condom won't cover lesions that appear on his scrotum or testicles. So abstaining from sex is sometimes the best thing to do.

The Social Repercussions of an STI

I ended up confronting Derek. I felt he needed to know what he had done, so he would use a condom from then on. We dated for a little while longer. Then he decided to go back to his ex-girlfriend. We're no longer friends.

Each day, I try to deal with the fact that I have herpes. And when people put me down or treat me like I'm different, it makes coping with it even harder. Herpes has especially changed my life when it comes to relationships. You never know when you're supposed to tell someone and if they will freak out.

After I was diagnosed, I started dating an old boyfriend again. When I told him about it, he acted like he was fine with it. But the next day, he started being really distant. Then I found out he told a lot of people, which really hurt. Whenever someone acted weird toward me, I wondered if it was because they knew.

One time, my old boyfriend's friend was in class with me and started talking really loudly about me to another person in the room. "Yeah, she's a whore and has herpes from some guy she knew for like an hour," he said. "Guess that taught her to keep her legs shut." I had to leave the room I was crying so hard.

Being Honest and Being Safe

When I first got the virus, I thought, "Who would want to ever marry a girl with herpes?"

But the more I am open with people about it, the more I learn that it's OK. I know that someone will love me for me and not care that I have herpes, because the virus doesn't make me who I am. Still, sometimes I avoid relationships altogether, for fear of rejection. And that makes me lonely.

So, think about my story when you're having sex. Ask your future partners the hard questions, too. Ask them about their sexual past, when they were tested, for what, and, since then, what they've done to protect themselves.

And think about my story when you hear that someone has an STD. Most likely, if they have one, they are scared and lonely, and could use a friend.

My Life as a Teenage Mom

Amy Benfer

At 16, Amy Benfer decided to keep her four-day-old daughter, rather than give her up for adoption (as had been her plan), despite acknowledging that it likely would be healthier for her daughter to be raised by a married couple. With the help of her family, Benfer finished high school and college, and went on to live and work in Connecticut, San Francisco, and New York, without ever forgoing any of her dreams for her own future. Benfer recognizes her decision was radically selfish and based more on her own willfulness and self-image than any rational assessment of what was best for her or her daughter. Despite all of that, she has no regrets. Amy Benfer is a freelance writer. She lives in Brooklyn with her teenage daughter.

My daughter was 4 days old on the day I decided to be her parent. My father was in the driver's seat. I was a 16-year-old leaking milk in the back seat of my parents' station wagon when I made the announcement: "Let's go get her."

"We're going to get the baby," my father said, and drove over a wall of traffic cones to cross over into the turn lane. And that was that: Me, my parents, my younger brother, all of us went on this reckless mission to pick up a newborn baby we'd left with my mother's single friend until we figured out what the hell to do with her. I don't know how my father got there without killing us all. We were all crying. We knew it was a stupid idea. We knew we could be seriously messing up at least two lives. We knew that there was a perfectly appropriate adoptive couple, of the right age and financial situation, with a mortgage, two cars and a nursery waiting for that baby.

Amy Benfer, "Parenting on a Dare," *Salon*, May 10, 2003. This article first appeared in Salon.com, at http://www.salon.com. An online version remains in the *Salon* archives. Reprinted with permission.

But somehow we all rushed into the friend's condo, claimed our baby, and took her home, where she went to sleep in a tiny crib that had housed my baby dolls not that many years before.

We all made promises to that child. My brother, who was 10 at the time, promised to donate all of his allowance for the next eight years, and a new pair of Bugle Boy jeans if we'd keep her. (We still haven't collected on that part of the deal, but I remind him every few years that coming through with at least the Bugle Boys is the right thing to do.) My parents promised to get me somehow to adulthood, by providing us both with a place to live and health insurance, giving me free childcare (from my stay-at-home mother) through high school and sending me on to college, as they had already planned to do.

Parenting on a Dare

My promise was the most complicated. On the morning my daughter was born, the doctor came in to talk to me. He knew my age. He knew there was an adoptive family waiting to take her (the bouquet they sent was on my nightstand). He knew I had not yet made the decision.

He told me that he was concerned with taking care of his patients' minds as well as their bodies. He said that, of course, the best decision for my daughter would be to place her for adoption. But, he said, perhaps I was not strong enough to make that choice.

My response? *F--- you.*

My doctor meant well, as did everyone else who had said more or less the same thing throughout my pregnancy. And I was the kind of girl that everyone believed would recognize that parenting my daughter as a teenager was not in the best interest of myself or my child.

But I took it as a dare. I had a 16-year-old's immortality complex. Up until then, nothing had been hard. I had had a safe, middle-class childhood in which the only dangers were those I got myself into—by, say, taking the family car in the middle of the night, or having sex.

Theorizing Why Teen Mothers Fail

I hated my doctor for implying, or so I thought, that keeping my child would be a sentimental decision made out of emotional weakness. To me, this was my chance to prove just how tough I was. Like most ambitious teenagers, I still believed at that time that I could choose between, you know, being president, winning the Pulitzer Prize for fiction (maybe poetry, maybe both) and maybe being a movie star or something in my youth. I was still going to do all that, and I was going to do it with a child. It was my chance to be extraordinary in the most literal sense, by breaking out of the ordinary college, career, dating, marriage, children trajectory that was expected of girls like me.

So my promise, to myself and my daughter, was that we were going to prove everyone wrong. I was going to raise a child who was every bit as smart, capable and badass as I thought I was. And I was going to do everything I would have done anyway, and do it just as well as, if not better than, I would have on my own.

My mother and I, both of us big talkers, would have long, ponderous discussions on why, exactly, teenage mothers often did badly. We didn't know many of them at all, and none intimately. We came up with theories, some more crackpot than others. We took our cues from novels, from people around us, from pop psychology. Of course, there was the money thing and the education thing. But we wanted to understand the psychology of teen parenting. One of us—I'm not sure which one—came up with the idea that teenage mothers were often emotionally stunted at the age when they first became pregnant, because, as we decided, they hadn't "gone through all their developmental stages."

It was an arrogant pronouncement, one that certainly revealed that neither one of us had much experience with any situations that fell outside the range of typical family life, the kind of life we had just agreed that I was going to have.

Making Selfishness a Moral Imperative

I took it to mean that, at 16, I should act like a 16-year-old; at 18, like an 18-year-old; at 25, like a 25-year-old, and so on. The danger, as we saw it, was that if I gave up too much of my own identity into being a mother at a young age, I would resent my child and that would be a bad thing.

In other words, being a good mother, for me, was entirely dependent on how good I was at taking care of myself. I not only gave myself license to be selfish, but following my selfish instincts also became a moral imperative.

For the first two years of my daughter's life, my parents insulated me from the usual consequences of teenage motherhood. There was no question that I was my daughter's parent, but I certainly was not a single parent. My mother did the childcare from 8 a.m. to 3 p.m.; my father earned the income. My job was to do well in school and to enjoy my baby. And since my job was also to be a "normal" high school girl, I also went out with friends and to punk rock shows on the weekends after my daughter was asleep and to poetry club at the coffeehouse every two weeks. I was too busy to date much until the end of my senior year, but if I'd wanted to, I could have done that too.

Because it was so easy, I got bolder. The first major conflict between my parents' generosity and my own ambitions came around the time I started to apply to college. My parents, who had both gone to state schools, had once been perfectly happy to send me to whatever private school I wanted to attend. They still agreed that I should go to college, but they wanted to keep me close to home where they could help out. I saw no reason why I should scale back my ambitions just because I had a child. I applied to all the same schools I would have anyway and finally chose a very expensive school 3,000 miles away from home.

I Have Never Returned Home

My parents were horrified, but in the end, they didn't stop me. I don't think anyone could have. When they said it was too expensive, I asked for their tax returns and suggested ways they could meet the expected parental contribution. When they worried about how we would live, I called the dean of my school and came back with childcare, a two-bedroom apartment, and a meal plan for us both. Two years later, when they told me they could not afford to pay for that school, I took a year off and went back as an independent student. My daughter and I moved to Connecticut when I was 18, and, except for brief visits back, I have never gone home again.

Every few years, I try to write an essay with the working title "Without You." It's supposed to be a piece that follows the imaginary person in my head, the version of myself who has lived a parallel life without taking that dare and deciding to raise a child at 16. I've never been able to write that story. Part of it must be that having a child shapes every part of a person's identity, so that it becomes impossible to imagine a self who has not been formed by taking care of that child. But the other reason I've never been able to write that story is that having a child didn't change me *enough*.

This year, I will have been a mother for exactly half my life. I'll turn 30 in less than a month; my daughter will turn 14 this summer. If you had asked me at 15 what I saw myself doing at 30, I would probably have said that I would be a writer living in New York. And, at 30, I live in Brooklyn and have made my living as a writer for nearly seven years. At 18, I was an English major at a college I loved. At 23, I moved to San Francisco to be near my boyfriend, a brilliant novelist whom I loved. At 25, I had my dream job as an editor at *Sa-*

lon (which, yes, I also love). And at 29, I moved to New York, where I am still doing work that I love. I'm not going to pretend that I couldn't write another version of my life about all the ways I've failed to get and do what I want. But it's difficult to believe that the bare outline of my life for the past 15 years would look any different if I'd had the freedom to construct it without taking my child into consideration.

What My Daughter Didn't Have

I kept the first part of my promise to myself: Being a parent didn't stop me from doing what I wanted to do. The second part, is, of course, my promise to my daughter. Fifteen years after she was conceived, do I think I did right by her? The worst part of being the parent of older children is that you see the effects of everything you have done. You know exactly how you have damaged your child, in the same way that you know exactly how your own parents have damaged you. It's a cost/benefit analysis. I don't always know what she thinks of me, but I know what kind of parent I am. I still have a nearly subhuman immunity to risk. After making the decision to raise a child at 16, few things compare. Nothing seems crazy to me. I am a warm parent. I love to talk to my daughter. But I'm also undisciplined. I'm messy. I'm selfish. We've never had enough money, enough space, enough time. When I fail—to clean the apartment, to meet a deadline, to find a job, to keep a lover—I have the same tendency to think *f--- you*. You try to raise a child on your own at 16 (at 22, 25, 29). It's an excuse. People let me use it more often than they should.

I am in the strange situation of having known the couple who wanted to raise my child if I had not chosen to do so. I selected them, I sat in their living room, I toured the house and talked with them about their philosophy of child-rearing. We haven't spoken in 15 years, but I've heard enough to have an idea of where they are now. I know that in her parallel life, my child would have grown up the daughter of a social worker and a real estate agent in the Northwest. She would live in a four-bedroom house; she would have a summer cottage in the mountains. She would have been allowed to have a dog, and it's likely she'd have a brother and a sister. She wouldn't have seen as much of the world. She may have grown up to be more like the girl I was at her age, a suburban teenager longing for adventure and danger and a more exciting life. She would have been more stable.

When a Terrible Idea Is Exactly Right

I don't know that girl. She isn't my daughter. The girl who is my daughter has been told her whole life that we almost didn't do it, that we almost lost our nerve. She knows as well as we do that was the sensible thing to do, and we haven't tried to hide it. As she's gotten older, she and I sometimes talk about what her life could have been like. She can't really imagine it, of course, any more than I can. I have an odd little line that I trot out sometimes. When she says she was an "accident," I tell her that she should feel that she is all the more a wanted child. We didn't want a child, I say, we wanted *you*. She wasn't convenient, she wasn't planned, she profoundly changed all of our lives. And we did it anyway.

I say "we" because I am thinking of the four of us in that station wagon, running over traffic cones on our way to do something that everyone else knew was a terrible idea. And you know what? We were exactly, exactly right.

A Doctor's Perspective on Teen Pregnancy

Barbara J. Howard

Barbara J. Howard is an assistant professor of pediatrics at Johns Hopkins University, Baltimore, and codirector of the Center for Promotion of Child Development through Primary Care. She is the author of hundreds of articles, monographs, book chapters, and instructional videos, and has served on numerous editorial boards. In this article she advises doctors on how best to approach teen pregnancy in their practice, especially the first, often emotional, step of informing a teen and her family of the pregnancy and beginning to explore options. Howard highlights the importance of being sensitive to the teen's emotions and autonomy in decision making, underscoring that, whether the young woman chooses to terminate or continue the pregnancy, immediate action needs to be taken to protect the patient's health.

Teenage pregnancy is on the decline in our country, but it's still remarkably common, with 750,000 adolescents aged 15–19 years becoming pregnant each year.

Of course, we'd like to prevent those pregnancies that are unwanted, but the odds are not always on our side. A sexually active young woman who does not use contraception has a 90% chance of becoming pregnant in 1 year. And even though the majority of adolescents are waiting until they are a little older to have sex these days and using contraception when they do, contraceptive use is not consistent, reflecting adolescents' developmental sense of invulnerability.

When a teenager in my practice turns up pregnant, I have to be careful. My first reaction is often anger or disappoint-

Barbara J. Howard, "Dealing With Teenage Pregnancy," *Pediatric News*, vol. 41, June 2007, pp. 34–35. Copyright 2007 International Medical News Group. Reproduced by permission.

ment, since I see prevention of teen pregnancy as an important part of my role as a pediatrician. Seeing a positive pregnancy test can make me feel like I've failed.

Be Sensitive to Her Feelings

I work hard, though, to hide my personal reactions to a pregnant teen. It's about her, after all, not about me.

I have to recognize that the way I view teen pregnancy as a married, white, educated professional woman and physician may not reflect the cultural norms of young women in the community I serve, where teenage pregnancy may be the norm, and even a welcome sign of maturity, fertility, and independence. Some mothers expect to raise their daughters' first babies, just as their own mothers did when they became pregnant at 16. Rates of teen pregnancies are highly variable. In Baltimore, for example, half of first pregnancies are in mothers 19 and under. From a strictly biological point of view, this is a great age to bear children.

In most cases, the news of a pregnancy is not cause for celebration in the pediatrician's office, and I like to be ready for what may be an emotional encounter. When a teenaged girl comes in and says, "I've been awfully tired lately," or presents with symptoms of a urinary tract infection, abdominal pain, breast tenderness, menstrual irregularity, or vaginal bleeding, it's a tip-off to me to make sure I get that patient alone as soon as I can. In many states, a sexually active teenager is a legally emancipated minor with the right to complete decision-making and confidential care. These rights are hard to provide if the teen's mother remains in the room as the possibility of pregnancy is broached and the telltale results of a pregnancy test arrive.

Empower Her to Make Decisions

I think it's much better to share the news with the teenager alone, so I can ask her, "How are you going to talk to your parents about this?" If she is reluctant to tell her parents by herself, I offer to help her break the news with her in the room, or, if she requests, to tell the parents myself with her out of the room. Whether the teen is present or not, I try to shape the conversation to accept parental anger but move on quickly to teamwork. "Obviously, this is a big moment in your teen's life," I might say. "How would you like to come out of this in terms of her relationship with you?" I've had parents who scream at me and cry for half an hour before they can face their teenager calmly. Serving that role is OK with me. I want to make sure the teenager is safe and supported during this difficult time.

Note that I do not encourage the possibility that my patient will not confide the news to her parents, although each case is different. Sometimes when an adolescent says, "My parents are going to kill me," the potential for physical harm is real. In these rare instances, I do whatever I can to help her find resources independently.

In any case, it is the teen's decision whether and when to tell her family. Maintain confidentiality by being careful what you write on the diagnosis sheet if the bill is going to her parents. She may want to pay for the pregnancy test herself to avoid revealing the situation before she is ready.

As pediatricians, we represent authority figures to teenagers. They may be afraid of our reactions, as well as those of their parents. I try to make it clear that I am here to be an advocate, offering objective but compassionate assistance for whatever decision she makes. I try to convey this through every pore of my being, and I do believe that if physicians are not comfortable being objective, they need to know ahead of time how to refer teens to someone who is. Planned Parenthood is an excellent resource—accessible in most communities—that provides adoption or abortion counseling and early prenatal care if she decides to keep the baby.

Assess Her Relationship and Safety

I always ask teenagers, "What do you think your partner is going to think of this pregnancy?" It's an important question for the answers it may reveal. Was this young woman having sex in an attempt to provide herself with self-esteem and comfort because she is depressed? Was she the victim of incest or date rape, or taken advantage of sexually in any way? How old is this partner? I get very concerned about coercive relationships if I hear that the partner is any more than 2–3 years older than she is.

Assess your patient's psychological well-being at this time, making sure she is not vulnerable to self-harm.

Ask whether she has thought about what she is going to do. Some teens have thought about this in detail already and expected a positive test. Still, I think it is good to view the situation through the prism of the four domains of adolescent strengths and development outlined in "Bright Futures in Practice, Mental Health": belonging, independence, mastery, and generosity. Keep in mind how the teen's behavior, strengths, and weaknesses fall into these categories. For example, you might explain that one young woman's drive to create an independent life and sense of belonging to a new family with her partner is actually appropriate for her age and that she has the generous qualities of a good mother. Also discuss the other skills she has mastered, evidenced by her good grades in school and college plans, and encourage her to consider how a choice of keeping this baby might influence these ambitions. Going through these domains will make it possible for teenagers to hear you, because you are touching on strengths they care about rather than telling them what to do.

Inform Her of Options

Educate teenagers about their options, which include abortion, adoption, and keeping their babies. Statistics show that 57% of teens choose abortion, 29% give birth, and 14% miscarry. You should ensure that they have access to accurate information about each possibility, but keep in mind that you'll need to follow up, and follow up quickly.

The window for an abortion is narrow, and teens choosing to keep their babies need access to prenatal care as early as possible. I always specify that they should not drink, smoke, or use any drugs or medicines while they are deciding. I think this makes the responsibilities of pregnancy more real as well as beginning to protect the fetus.

I either schedule a follow-up appointment or call teens within a few days to see how they are doing with their decision, how they're doing with their families, and how I can help. Keep the door open to your young and vulnerable patients during this time, both for their well-being now and to promote thoughtful decisions later about their reproductive health.

My Relationship with an Older Woman

Ariel Levy

Ariel Levy is a contributing editor for New York *magazine and author of the book* Female Chauvinist Pigs: Women and the Rise of Raunch Culture. *Her writing explores sexuality, gender roles, and the status of modern feminism in U.S. popular culture. From her 2006 article exploring relationships between older professional women and teenage boys, Levy recounts the stories of women who have pursued teenage boys sexually. These stories call attention to a predicament that many young men fall into, caught between the mass-media fantasy of being sexually admired by an older woman and yet being a young person manipulated into having sex.*

The older woman. Knowledgeable, seasoned, experienced. Hot! The fantasy creature who embodies full-blown female sexuality in all its mysterious glory. Of course, she's out of reach; it will never happen. She inhabits her own complicated realm of emotions and responsibilities and lingerie, and you are just . . . a kid. But imagine the initiation! The possibilities! (Sexually, sure, but also for bragging.) It would be awesome.

Or would it? What if the impossible happened and she started paying unmistakably romantic attention to you. What if "she told me that she had feeling for me. She told me that she was thinking about me a lot and had feeling for me [and] she didn't know what to do with them," as 24-year-old Debra Lafave told one of her 14-year-old pupils, according to his statement to the police. What if you had sex in the classroom?

What if she fell in love with you? What if she wanted to marry you? If it stopped being a fantasy and started being your actual sex life, your actual life, would it be thrilling or upsetting? Or both? Would you be scarred for life or psyched for months?

These are questions we've had plenty of opportunities to contemplate lately. A few months ago, 37-year-old Lisa Lynette Clark pleaded guilty to statutory rape of her son's 15-year-old close friend, whom Clark married and whose child she recently gave birth to. In January, a 26-year-old math teacher from Kentucky named Angela Comer was arrested in Mexico with one of her eighth-grade male students (who had allegedly stolen $800 from his grandmother for trip money). They had been trying to get married.

Dirty old(er) women do not reside exclusively in states with alligator problems; we have our fair share in the New York area. In August, Sandra Beth Geisel, a former Catholic-school teacher and the wife of a prominent banker in Albany, was sentenced to six months in jail for having sex with a 16-year-old, and she has admitted to sleeping with two of her 17-year-old pupils. (The presiding judge in the case infuriated the youngest boy's parents when he told Geisel her actions were illegal but that her youngest sexual partner "was certainly not victimized by you in any other sense of the word.") In October, Lina Sinha, an administrator and a former teacher at Manhattan Montessori on East 55th Street, was charged with second- and third-degree sodomy and third-degree rape for allegedly having sex with a former student—who is now a cop—for four years starting when he was 13 and she was 29 (she denies the charges). And last May, Christina Gallagher, a 25-year-old Spanish teacher from Jersey City, pleaded guilty to second-degree sexual assault of a 17-year-old male student.

The story that probably set the most imaginations in motion is Lafave's. Debra Lafave, a 24-year-old middle-school teacher who looks like a Miss America contestant, is currently serving three years under house arrest for having sex repeatedly with one of her 14-year-old male students. After a hearing, Lafave's lawyer, John Fitzgibbons, notoriously said that his client, a former model, was too pretty for jail: "[T]o place an attractive young woman in that kind of hellhole is like putting a piece of raw meat in with the lions." As in several of the other cases, Lafave's beauty and youth blurred the lines of her narrative. What were these stories about? We couldn't tell if they were instances of abuse by adults in positions of power who were badly harming children or if they were American Pie/Maxim magazine-style farces about lucky little dudes.

When I was growing up, my father used to say as a joke (sort of), "Teenage boys: the lowest form of life on earth." He was probably imagining some combination of his adolescent self and Philip Roth's Alexander Portnoy, a character who revolved around a tight coil of urge and surge and shame, whose repertoire of obsessions ranged from onanism to defilement and whose actions seemed almost piteously in thrall to his loins rather than his head (which was too busy processing anxiety and guilt to offer much guidance). Portnoy's Complaint was a best seller in 1967, but to this day its protagonist is for many people besides my father the epitome of adolescent-male sexuality: desperate, reckless, insatiable. The horny little devil.

If you conceive of teenage boys as walking heaps of lust, you probably conceive of attractive adult teachers who hit on them as public servants in more ways than one.

Media representations of grown women who pursue teenage boys have hardly been scary in recent years. Phoebe's brother on Friends married his home-ec teacher and proceeded to live happily ever after. Jennifer Aniston's affair with little love-struck Jake Gyllenhaal in *The Good Girl* would be difficult to describe as abuse. He pined for her, he worshipped her, and if he ended up destroyed, we couldn't blame her . . . a lost little girl who happened to be in her thirties.

The most famous older woman is, of course, Mrs. Robinson: sinister as well as smoldering, coolly and mercilessly manipulating Benjamin to get what she wants and keep what he wants out of reach. But the fictional figure who is really more representative of our stereotypes is Blanche DuBois in *A Streetcar Named Desire*. Tennessee Williams made her a skittering, simpering hysteric. Where Mrs. Robinson unfurls her silk stocking with utter confidence in her own allure and smoky erotic power, Blanche rushes to cover the lightbulb with a paper lantern so nobody will see the years creeping over her face. (For the record, her advanced age was 30.) She is desperate for attention and dependent upon the "kindness of strangers," and, it is suggested, she hit on her 17-year-old male student because her own maturity was stunted and only a young boy would make an appropriate companion for the young girl still living within her withering skin. By the end of that play, she is raped by Stanley Kowalski, then carted off to the loony bin: a victim.

It's jarring, however, to think of a teenage boy—say, a 16-year-old—who's been seduced by a female teacher as a victim. It clashes with our assumptions. A teenage boy who gets to live his fantasy? What can be the harm?

As it happens, that is a very dangerous question. In 1998, Bruce Rind, Philip Tromovitch, and Robert Bauserman (professors at Temple University, the University of Pennsylvania, and the University of Michigan, respectively) published a study that has resounded through the psychological Establishment ever since. The article, published in the *American Psychological Association's Psychological Bulletin*, was what's known as a meta-analysis, an overview of the existing science, in this case on the long-term effects of childhood sexual abuse. The authors concluded that "negative effects were neither pervasive nor typically intense" and that men who'd been abused "reacted much less negatively than women."

Though Rind and his colleagues bent over backward to emphasize the difference between something's being wrong and something's being harmful (it's wrong, for instance, to shoot a gun at someone, even if you miss), the study was spectacularly demonized. Dr. Laura Schlessinger had three psychologists on her show who declared it "junk science." One of them compared its authors to Nazi doctors. The Alaska State Legislature passed a resolution condemning the study's conclusions and methodologies. In May 1999, the Family Research Council along with Tom DeLay held a press conference in Washington demanding the APA retract the Rind study. (Schlessinger was teleconferenced in.)

About a year after the study's publication, Congress passed a formal resolution condemning Rind in an uncontested vote. The president of the APA initially defended the paper and pointed out that it had been peer-reviewed and determined to be scientifically sound, but as the resolution was being debated, he sent a clarification to DeLay saying that child sexual abuse was always harmful and—though the study has never been scientifically discredited—the organization has been trying to distance itself from Rind ever since.

Although it is tempting to assume that the finding that childhood sexual abuse is not as damaging for boys as for girls confirms various widely held beliefs about gender—that boys are tougher and hornier than girls, that males enjoy sex in any form—the issue is more complicated. For one thing, when men seek out sex with underage girls, they are more likely than their female counterparts to have more than one victim and to utilize methods like coercion and threats to secure complicity and secrecy. Women who seek sex with underage boys are more likely to focus on one person and to proffer love and loyalty and a sense of a particular and profound bond. In many of these cases, the woman has floated the idea of marriage.

We (Still) like to keep our understanding of masculinity connected to our understanding of maturity. We'd never had a female anchorwoman deliver our news until recently, we don't often let female columnists explain the news, and we've never had a female president to make the news. For many Americans, being a real grown-up requires a penis. And if you've got that, even if you're only 15, you must have the maturity and the manliness to know what you want to do with it—even if that involves intercourse with a 42-year-old. Who among us would say the same thing about a 15-year-old girl?

"For guys, the different issue than for young women is that it's supposed to be the best thing anybody could want in terms of what society is saying or their friends," says Lonnie Barbach, a clinical psychologist and the author of *The Erotic Edge*. "But they don't necessarily feel okay about it, so then they're acting against their feelings. I see a lot of guys with sexual problems who've had that experience. Problems with erections are pretty common, as is anxiety around sex in general." But then, she points out, she only sees the ones who have problems.

It's extremely common for boys who have been molested to be drawn exclusively to much older women from then on. "There is something about early experience with sexuality that tends to stay with you," Barbach says. "A lot of it is by chance. If you are a child who stumbled upon a magazine with women who have very large breasts, you may eroticize women who look like that in adulthood. It's funny, I don't know why it is, but as a child you are just more susceptible." Anything sexual that happens in childhood has a better chance of making a kind of imprint on your erotic consciousness.

Even if we take as a given that it's always wrong for a grown woman to have sex with her teenage students, or her son's friend, or whatever other 15-year-old she gets her hands on, a question still remains: Why would she want to in the first place?

Teenage boys are not, as a rule, the world's most expert lovers. They are not known for their emotional sophistication or sensitivity. And they do not excel at the tests of masculine status women are supposed to be fixated upon. "If Debra had had an affair with a man who was richer than me, or more successful, that I could have understood," as Debra Lafave's estranged husband, Owen, put it. "But this was a boy. What could he offer her that I couldn't?"

Power, for one thing. Compared with a teenage boy, a woman will almost always make more money. She will always know more about sex. She will generally be more competent and experienced and more able to assert her will on him than vice versa.

If you spend a little time going over stories of grown women who pursue boys, they start to blur together. Often, the woman was a victim of sexual abuse in her own childhood. So in some cases adults' having sex with children is familiar, reiterative. Psychologists say one reason women engage in this is to create a new narrative: If they as adults can have sex with a child in the context of a loving romance (imaginary or real) rather than as an obvious enactment of exploitation, they can then more easily conceive of their own abuse as a love story. To them, the experience of being a gentle perpetrator can be redemptive.

"Sometimes, the woman is not much older psychologically than the boy is in her developmental stage," says clinical psychologist Judy Kuriansky. "She has arrested development. So she's having sex with a 14-year-old, and in her head, she's 14, too. She's getting the attention she never got." She's Blanche DuBois. And, Kuriansky says, "there's nothing more erotic that being adored, for women."

Consider the poster couple for pedophilia or true love, depending on your point of view: Mary Kay Letourneau and Vili Fualaau. A review: Letourneau was Fualaau's second-grade teacher, then she taught him again—and had sex with him—

when he was a 12-year-old in her sixth-grade class. She gave birth to their first child shortly before she went to jail. She became pregnant with their second child when she was out on parole. She went back to jail for seven years. After her release, they got back together. Letourneau and Fualaau were married in a televised ceremony last May and registered for china at Macy's. They have been together ten years.

You could clearly hear Letourneau imbuing her student with power; trying to convince the public as she'd convinced herself that Fualaau—her lover, her hero—was on more than equal footing with her: "He dominated me in the most masculine way that any man, any leader, could do."

He was 12. She was 34.

When Diane Demartini-Scully first started going for walks with her daughter's 15-year-old boyfriend on the North Fork of Long Island, it made him feel special. "She would just talk to me about life situations and shit," he says now, a year and a half later. "It was pretty cool." This is something DeMartini-Scully, a 45-year-old blonde who vaguely resembles Erica Jong, would have been good at. She was, until recently, a school psychologist at East Hampton Middle School. She knew how to draw a kid out.

And the boy, let's call him Jason, had some things on his mind. "I was making a lot of money in New York," he says, and when I ask him how, he gives a nervous laugh. "I was doing a lot of things." I ask if the things he was doing and the company he was keeping (mostly in Jamaica, Queens, he says) were part of the reason his family left Mattituck, Long Island, where they lived just down the road from DeMartini-Scully, for Jacksonville, North Carolina, where they currently reside. He says yes, but the reason his mother has given the press for the move was to escape the escalating cost of living on the North Fork. Detective Steven L. Harned of the local Southold Police Department says, "We were already aware of [Jason]. He has had some court cases here on other matters."

When Jason's family was ready to relocate to Jacksonville, he still had a few months of school remaining. It was decided that Jason would finish off the year living at DeMartini-Scully's house on Donna Drive. "We would go to Blockbuster and rent movies, and when we watched them, she would put her hand on my lap," Jason says. "I didn't think much of it at the time."

One night, when DeMartini-Scully's daughter, with whom Jason was still involved, was at a friend's house, and after DeMartini-Scully's son had gone to sleep, she asked Jason if he wanted to watch television with her in her bed. "Then she kissed me."

That night, Jason and DeMartini-Scully "basically did everything." He remembers the experience as "okay . . . I wouldn't say it was upsetting. I wouldn't say I didn't want to, but . . . I figured she was letting me stay at her house, I'd just do what she wanted."

This was not an isolated incident. For the next three and a half months, Jason estimates, the two continued having sex at the house and in her car. "Nobody suspected anything," he says. "And I didn't want nobody to know because I was messing around with her daughter. I found it funny that Diane was letting me stay at her house when she knew about that, but I never asked her why: I figured she was doing it because she wanted something."

I ask Jason what he wanted: whether he was having sex with DeMartini-Scully because he enjoyed it or because he felt obliged to. "When I wasn't drunk, I felt pressured to, but when I was drunk, I wanted to . . . you know what I mean?" He claimed he got alcohol, and sometimes pot, from DeMartini-Scully.

When summer came, DeMartini-Scully took her son and daughter and Jason down to Florida, where they met up with Jason's family for a vacation en route to Jacksonville. What was supposed to be a quick stop to see Jason's family's new house became an extended stay when DeMartini-Scully was injured in an accident. "She hurt her leg pretty bad when I was teaching her how to ride the dirt bike," Jason says. "You could see her bone and shit." She stayed in North Carolina for a month.

When she finally left, Jason's mother was glad to be rid of DeMartini-Scully. She had become suspicious when she found out that Jason and DeMartini-Scully had been in a room with the door locked. But on Columbus Day weekend, unbeknownst to Jason's mother, DeMartini-Scully returned to a hotel in Jacksonville to visit Jason. "So I want to know, what's so special about me?" Jason says. I ask him what he thinks. He laughs. "I'm not gonna say."

He spent three days at the hotel. His mother found out about the visit, and "that's when all the drama started." She contacted the police, who charged DeMartini-Scully with kidnapping and providing marijuana to a minor but not with sexual assault, because Jason had, at this point, already turned 16 and passed the legal age of consent in North Carolina. She was subsequently charged with third-degree rape and performing a criminal sexual act in Suffolk County, where the age of consent is 17.

Jason stayed in school for just three weeks in Jacksonville before he dropped out. He says he will join the Marines after he gets his GED, "but just for the money." He doesn't miss DeMartini-Scully, he says, who by the end was suggesting she wanted to marry him. But he also says he doesn't feel raped. "I just, I don't know, I feel weird. She was 30 years older than me, so I feel a little bit taken advantage of. If I was a girl, I probably wouldn't talk to you about it, but a female can't really rape a guy, you know?"

Jason says he would not have given a statement to the Long Island police incriminating DeMartini-Scully if he hadn't been under pressure. "They said if I didn't they were gonna press charges on me because I was with Diane's daughter," who is only 14, and now Jason is 17, thus making him guilty of "sexual misconduct" himself. As of his last birthday, Jason's relationships switched status in the eyes of the law: Sex with the then-44-year-old school psychologist who had been after him since he was 16 became okay; sex with her teenage daughter became a crime.

("It is a strange law," says Harned. "I didn't write them, I just enforce them." Harned says that it is still likely that the Southold Police Department will press charges against Jason for his relationship with the daughter and that Jason was not pushed into giving a statement about the mother.)

"I just think about how Diane's daughter must feel now," Jason says. "I was pretty close to her; I still am. I'm talking to her on the computer right now."

I ask Jason if this is an experience he will try to avoid in the future, getting involved with much older women. He thinks about it for a minute. "Depends how old," he concludes. "How old are you?"

Organizations to Contact

The editors have compiled the following list of organizations concerned with the issues presented in this book. The descriptions are derived from materials provided by the organizations. The list was compiled on the date of publication of the present volume; the information provided here may change. Be aware that many organizations take several weeks or longer to respond to inquiries, so allow as much time as possible.

Advocates for Youth
2000 M St. NW, Suite 750, Washington, DC   20036
202-419-3420 • fax: 202-419-1448
e-mail: info@advocatesforyouth
Web site: www.advocatesforyouth.org

Advocates for Youth supports programs that increase youths' opportunities and abilities to make healthy decisions about sexuality. It publishes a variety of fact sheets and reports, as well as *Transitions*, a quarterly newsletter for professionals and advocates.

The Alan Guttmacher Institute
125 Maiden Lane, New York, NY   10038
212-248-1111 • fax: 212-248-1951
e-mail: info@guttmacher.org
Web site: www.guttmacher.org

The Alan Guttmacher Institute works to protect and expand the reproductive choices of everyone. It strives to ensure people's access to the information and services they need to exercise their rights and responsibilities concerning sexual activity, reproduction, and family planning. Among the institute's publications are the books *Teenage Pregnancy in Industrialized Countries* and *Today's Adolescents, Tomorrow's Parents: A Portrait of the Americas* and the report *Sex and America's Teenagers*.

American Civil Liberties Union (ACLU)
125 Broad St., 18th Fl., New York, NY   10004
212-549-2500
e-mail: aclu@aclu.org
Web site: www.aclu.org

The ACLU is a national organization that works to defend Americans' civil rights guaranteed by the U.S. Constitution. The ACLU's Lesbian and Gay Rights/AIDS Project handles litigation, education, and public policy work on behalf of gays and lesbians. It publishes the semiannual newsletter *Civil Liberties Alert* as well as policy papers such as "Responsible Spending: Real Sex Ed. for Real Lives."

American Social Health Association (ASHA)
PO Box 13827, Research Triangle Park, NC   27709
919-361-8400 • fax: 919-361-8425
Web site: www.ashastd.org

ASHA is a nonprofit organization dedicated to stopping sexually transmitted diseases and their harmful consequences. It advocates increased federal funding for STD programs and sound public policies on STD control. The association maintains an online sexual health glossary and publishes a quarterly newsletter on herpes, the *Helper*. ASHA's Women's Health Program provides information on pelvic inflammatory disease, vaginitis, Pap tests, and the effects of herpes simplex and HIV testing on pregnancy.

Coalition for Positive Sexuality (CPS)
PO Box 77212, Washington, DC   20013-7212
773-604-1654
e-mail: www.positive.org
Web site: cps@positive.org

CPS is a grassroots volunteer group that joins local high school students with several national activist groups. Its purpose is to give teens vital information about sexuality and to facilitate dialogue in and out of the public schools on condom availability and sex education. CPS publishes the booklet *Just Say Yes!*, available in English and Spanish.

Family Research Council (FRC)
801 G St. NW, Washington, DC   20001
202-393-2100 • fax: 202-393-2134
Web site: www.frc.org

The Family Research Council is a conservative Christian nonprofit think tank and lobbying group that "champions marriage and family as the foundation of civilization, the seedbed of virtue, and the wellspring of society." The FRC offers free policy papers, fact sheets, commentaries, and legislative alerts through its Web site.

Focus on the Family
Colorado Springs, CO   80995
719-531-5181
Web site: www.family.org

Focus on the Family is an evangelical group based in the United States that is "dedicated to nurturing and defending families worldwide." This nonprofit organization actively promotes interdenominational work for a social conservative public policy. Its Web site provides articles, resources and help in six different areas: parenting, relationships and marriage, life challenges, faith, entertainment, and social issues.

Henry J. Kaiser Family Foundation
2400 Sand Hill Rd., Menlo Park, CA   94025
650-854-9400 • fax: 650-854-4800
Web site: www.kff.org

The Henry J. Kaiser Family Foundation is a U.S.-based, private nonprofit organization dedicated to providing the media, policy makers, healthcare workers, and the general public with reliable information and analysis on issues of public health. Unlike many similar foundations, the Kaiser Family Foundation develops and conducts all of its own research and analysis, often in conjunction with outside organizations. Its Web site hosts a large collection of publications, including the *2003 National Survey of Adolescents and Young Adults: Sexual Health Knowledge, Attitudes and Experiences; Parents, Children & Media*; and *SexSmarts*, an ongoing sexual health education partnership between the Kaiser Family Foundation and *Seventeen* magazine.

National Campaign to Prevent Teen Pregnancy
1776 Massachusetts Ave. NW, Suite 200
Washington, DC   20036
202-478-8500
e-mail: campaign@teenpregnancy.org
Web site: www.teenpregnancy.org

The mission of the National Campaign is to reduce teenage pregnancy by supporting values and stimulating actions that are consistent with a pregnancy-free adolescence. The campaign's goal is to reduce the pregnancy rate among teenage girls by one-third between 2006 and 2015. The campaign publishes pamphlets, brochures, and opinion polls such as *Copy That: Guidelines for Replicating Programs to Prevent Teen Pregnancy, By the Numbers: The Public Costs of Teen Childbearing*, and *It's a Guy Thing: Boys, Young Men, and Teen Pregnancy Prevention*.

Planned Parenthood Federation of America
434 West Thirty-third St., New York, NY   10001
212-541-7800 • fax: 212-245-1845
Web site: www.plannedparenthood.org

Planned Parenthood believes that all individuals should have access to comprehensive sexuality education in order to make decisions about their own fertility. It provides contraception, abortion, STI, and family planning services at clinics located throughout the United States. Among its extensive publications are the fact sheets *Support the Responsible Education about Life Act, Pregnancy and Childbearing Among U.S. Teens*, and *Reducing Teenage Pregnancy*.

Sex, etc.
Center for Applied Psychology, Rutgers University
Piscataway, NJ 08854
732-445-7929 • fax: 732-445-5333
e-mail: answered@rci.rutgers.edu
Web site: www.sexetc.org

Sex, etc., the award-winning sexual-health Web site, is run by the Center for Applied Psychology at Rutgers University. Written for, and primarily by, teens, *Sex, etc.* offers information on a variety of topics, including sex, relationships, gender-identity issues, contraception, STIs, emotional health, and abuse, and is best known for publishing first-person accounts written by teens about the realities of their sexual choices in their lives.

Sexuality Information and Education Council of the United States (SIECUS)
130 W. Forty-Second St., Suite 350
New York, NY 10036-7802
212-819-9770 • fax: 212-819-9776
e-mail: siecus@siecus.org
Web site: www.siecus.org

SIECUS is a clearinghouse for information on sexuality, with a special interest in sex education. It publishes sex education curricula, the bimonthly newsletter *SIECUS Report*, and fact sheets on sex education issues. Its articles, bibliographies, and book reviews often address the role of sex education in reducing and preventing teen sexual activity.

Teen-Aid
723 E. Jackson Ave., Spokane, WA 99207
509-482-2868
e-mail: teenaid@teen-aid.org
Web site: www.teen-aid.org

Teen-Aid is a not-for-profit corporation whose purpose is to promote premarital abstinence in schools through parent-teen communication. It teaches the skills needed to reinforce character and family values. The main curricula developed by Teen-Aid cover general and reproductive health, parenting skills, birth control information, refusal skills, sexually transmitted disease information, sexual harassment, abuse, and date rape. Teen-Aid has online publications that can be accessed through its Web site.

Bibliography

Books

Michael J. Basso   *The Underground Guide to Teenage Sexuality*, Minneapolis, MN: Fairview Press, 2003.

Heather Corinna   *S.E.X.: The All-You-Need-To-Know Progressive Sexuality Guide to Get You Through High School and College*, New York: Marlowe, 2007.

Deborah Davis   *You Look Too Young to Be a Mom: Teen Mothers Speak Out on Love, Learning, and Success*, New York: Perigree Books, 2004.

Miriam Grossman   *Unprotected: A Campus Psychiatrist Reveals How Political Correctness in Her Profession Endangers Every Student*, New York: Sentinel, 2007.

Kelly Huegel   *GLBTQ*, Minneapolis, MN: Free Spirit Publishing, 2003.

Kevin Jennings and Pat Shapiro   *Always My Child: A Parent's Guide to Understanding Your Gay, Lesbian, Bisexual, Transgendered or Questioning Son or Daughter*, Old Tappan, NJ: Fireside, 2002.

Judith Levine   *Harmful to Minors: The Perils of Protecting Children from Sex*. Minneapolis: University of Minnesota Press, 2002.

Roger W. Libby | *The Naked Truth about Sex: A Guide to Intelligent Sexual Choices for Teenagers and Twentysomethings,* Nashville, TN: Freedom Press, 2006.

Kristin Luker | *When Sex Goes to School: Warring Views on Sex—and Sex Education—Since the Sixties,* New York: Norton, 2007.

Meg Meeker | *Epidemic: How Teen Sex Is Killing Our Kids,* Washington, DC: LifeLine Press, 2002.

Richard A. Panzer | *Condom Nation: Blind Faith, Bad Science,* Westwood, NJ: Center for Educational Media, 1997.

Linda Ellen Perry | *How to Survive Your Teen's Pregnancy: Practical Advice for a Christian Family,* Dumfries, VA: Chalfont House, 2003.

Susan Pogany | *Sex Smart: 501 Reasons to Hold Off on Sex: A Sexuality Resource for Teenagers,* Minneapolis, MN: Fairview Press, 1998.

Paul C. Reisser | *Teen Health Guide: Focus on the Family Parents' Guide to Teen Health,* Wheaton, IL: Tyndale House, 2002.

Anna Runkle | *In Good Conscience: A Practical, Emotional and Spiritual Guide to Deciding Whether to Have an Abortion,* Hoboken, NJ: Jossey-Bass, 1998.

Ritch C.
Savin-Williams

Mom, Dad, I'm Gay. How Families Negotiate Coming Out, Washington, DC: American Psychological Association Books, 2001.

Joe White

Pure Excitement: A Radical Righteous Approach to Sex, Love, and Dating, Wheaton, IL: Tyndale House, 1996.

Periodicals

Robert Wm.
Bloom

"Adolescent Sexuality," *Washingtonpost.com*, May 16, 2006. Retrieved February 7, 2008 from http://www.washingtonpost.com/wp-dyn/content/discussion/2006/05/12/DI200605 1201149.html.

Sandra G.
Broodman

"Virginity Pledges Can't Be Taken on Faith," *Washington Post*, May 16, 2006.

Michelle Burford

"Girls and Sex: You Won't Believe What's Going On," *O, The Oprah Magazine*, November 2002.

John Cloud

"The Battle Over Gay Teens: What happens when you come out as a kid? How gay youths are challenging the right—and the left," *Time*, October 10, 2005.

Cynthia Dailard

"Legislating Against Arousal: The Growing Divide between Federal Policy and Teenage Sexual Behavior," *Guttmacher Policy Review*, Summer 2006.

Forbes   "4 in 10 Kids See Adult Material On-
                        line: Study," February 5, 2007.

Alison George   "Going All the Way: Do Teenagers
                        Need More Sex Education, or Less?"
                        New Scientist, March 5, 2005.

Nancy Gibbs   "Defusing the War Over the
                        'Promiscuity' Vaccine," *Time*, June 21,
                        2006.

Ellen Goodman   "Good News on Cancer? Not for Ev-
                        eryone," *Boston Globe*, November 12,
                        2005.

Jeff Grabmeier   "Early Sex May Lead Teens to Delin-
                        quency, Study Shows," *EurekaAlert!*,
                        February 26, 2007. Retrieved Febru-
                        ary 7, 2008, from http://
                        www.eurekalert.org/pub_releases/
                        2007-02/osu-esm022607.php.

Lev Grossman   "The Secret Love Lives of Teenage
                        Boys," *Time*, September 4, 2006.

Whitney Joiner   "I Hid My Pregnancy," *Seventeen*,
                        December 2006.

Michael D.   "A Teen Twist on Sex," *Time*, Septem-
Lemonick   ber 19, 2005.

Tamar Lewin   "Survey Shows Sex Practices of
                        Boys," *New York Times*, December 19,
                        2000.

Gregory Lopes   "HPV Vaccine Concerns Give Legisla-
                        ture Pause," *Knight Ridder/Tribune
                        Business News*, April 25, 2007.

Susan McClelland   "Not So Hot to Trot," *Maclean's*, April 9, 2001.

Mark O'Connell   "The Epidemic of Meaningless Teen Sex," *Boston Globe*, March 9, 2005.

Ruth Padawer   "Big Increase in Oral Sex Among Teens May Be Myth," *Record*, September 16, 2005.

Karen S. Peterson   "Younger Kids Trying It Now, Often Ignorant of Risks," *USA Today*, November 16, 2000.

Lisa Remez   "Oral Sex Among Adolescents: Is It Sex or Abstinence?" *Family Planning Perspectives*, November 2000.

William Saletan   "Vandals and Virgins," *Slate*, http://www.slate.com/toolbar.aspx?action=print&id=2177821, November 29, 2007.

Diana Jean Schemo   "Sex Education with Just One Lesson: No Sex," *New York Times*, December 28, 2000.

Diana Jean Schemo   "What Teenagers Talk About When They Talk About Chastity," *New York Times*, January 28, 2001.

Laura Sessions Stepp   "Study: Half of All Teens Have Had Oral Sex," *Washington Post*, September 16, 2005.

Laura Vanderkam   "Sexually Active Girls' Lament: Why Didn't I Wait?" *USA Today*, June 11, 2006.

Rick Weiss   "Study Debunks Theory on Teen Sex, Delinquency," *Washington Post*, November 11, 2007.

Cathy Young   "Double Standard: The Bias Against Male Victims of Sexual Abuse," *Reason*, June 4, 2002.

Index

transmission, 129
types, 129
HIV, 51, 103, 107, 113
Homosexuality, 26, 30, 46, 84–91, 97
  adolescent, 73
  appearance, 76
  behaviors, 76
  beliefs, 76
  coming out, 78
  community, 78
  consequences, 78
  culture, 83
  definitions, 77
  first impulse, 78
  hate crimes, 82
  identity, 75, 83
  political establishment, 73
  self-identification, 82
  teenagers, 74
Honesty, 17, 131
Howard, Barbara, 139–143
HPV (human papilloma virus), 58–60, 58–71, 64–65
Hypersexualization, 20
Hysteria, 115, 117

I

Identity, 73, 75–78, 80–81, 83, 95
Incest, 142
Initiation age, 23
Institute of Women and Child Health, Karolinska Institute, 17
Intervention, 106
Intimacy, 46, 122

J

Johns Hopkins University, 18, 139

K

Kaiser Family Foundation, 19
Klick, Jonathan, 114
Kuriansky, Judy, 117, 150

L

Labels, 73–83
Lafave, Debra, 144–146, 150
Lelchuk, Ilene, 121–125
Lerner, Sharon, 25–37
Lesbian Gay Bisexual Transgender (LGBT), 84–91
Lesions, 129
Letourneau, Mary, 150
Levitt, Steven, 114
Love, 46
Luadzers, Darcy, 123

M

Maher, Bridget, 38–52
Male satisfaction, 115
Mandate, 64
Maple Grove high school, 25–37
Market forces, 113
Marriage, 26, 41
Masturbation, 46
McIllhaney Jr., Joe, 119
Media
  exposure, 20
  fun, 20
  hypersexualization, 20
  influence, 44
  messaging, 20
  risk and, 20
Medical care, 17
  abortion, 24, 114, 139, 142
  assessment, 142
  choices, 142
  confidentiality, 141

decision making, 139
emotion, 139
empowerment, 140
information, 142
options, 142
patient decision-making, 140–141
patient safety, 142
pregnancy, 139–140
provider perspectives, 139–143
sensitivity, 140
teen autonomy, 139
Medical confidentiality, 141
Medical Institute for Sexual Health, 119
Megan, 97–99
Mendenhall, Elissa, 64–71
Michaud, Pierre-Andre, 16
Mixed messages, 16, 19–20
Moral imperative, 135
Morning-after pill, 17
Mortality rate, 42
Motherhood, 132–138, 134
Multiple partners, 43
Myths, 130

N

National Campaign to Prevent Teen Pregnancy, 18
National Center for Health Statistics, 44, 115, 118
National Survey of Family Growth, 123, 124
National Youth Risk Behavior Study, 123
Netherlands, 16
The New School, 25
New York (magazine), 144
Not Me, Not Now program, 49
Notification laws, 114
Nutrition, 50

O

O (magazine), 116
Oral sex
age, 112, 118
asymmetry, 116
choice, 112
craze, 112
danger, 119
disease, 113
education, 46
emotion, 121
epidemic myth, 117
federal funds, 19
fellatio, 115–116, 118
female degradation, 116
female victim, 120
frequency, 112, 119
by girls, 112
hysteria, 115, 117
incentives, 112
increase, 112
intimacy, 122
male satisfaction, 115
market forces, 113
non-sex, 115
parents and, 115, 119, 122
participation rate, 115, 118–119, 123, 125
parties, 116
penetration substitute, 113
pleasure, 119
pregnancy, 122
prevalence, 123
provider rate, 115
public, 116
recipient, 115
risk, 122
safety, 113
self-confidence, 122
shame, 97–99, 122, 125
unreciprocated, 119